At Issue

What Is the Impact of E-Waste?

Other Books in the At Issue Series:

At Issue

What Is the Impact of E-Waste?

Tamara Thompson, Book Editor

GREENHAVEN PRESS
A part of Gale, Cengage Learning

Detroit • New York • San Francisco • New Haven, Conn • Waterville, Maine • London

Elizabeth Des Chenes, *Managing Editor*

© 2012 Greenhaven Press, a part of Gale, Cengage Learning

Gale and Greenhaven Press are registered trademarks used herein under license.

For more information, contact:
Greenhaven Press
27500 Drake Rd.
Farmington Hills, MI 48331-3535
Or you can visit our Internet site at gale.cengage.com

For product information and technology assistance, contact us at

Gale Customer Support, 1-800-877-4253
For permission to use material from this text or product, submit all requests online at www.cengage.com/permissions

Further permissions questions can be emailed to permissionrequest@cengage.com

Articles in Greenhaven Press anthologies are often edited for length to meet page requirements. In addition, original titles of these works are changed to clearly present the main thesis and to explicitly indicate the author's opinion. Every effort is made to ensure that Greenhaven Press accurately reflects the original intent of the authors. Every effort has been made to trace the owners of copyrighted material.

Cover image copyright © Debra Hughes 2007. Used under license from Shutterstock.com.

LIBRARY OF CONGRESS CATALOGING-IN-PUBLICATION DATA

What is the impact of e-waste? / Tamara Thompson, editor.
    p. cm. -- (At issue)
    Summary: "What Is the Impact of E-Waste?: Electronic Waste: An Overview; Planned Obsolescence Creates Unnecessary E-Waste; Developing Countries Are A Dumping Ground for Hazardous E-Waste; Illegal E-Waste from America Poisons Communities Overseas; Cell Phones Create Especially Problematic E-Waste; Prison Recycling Programs Are Dangerous for Inmates; Manufacturers Should Be Responsible for the E-Waste Their Products Generate; Consumers Should Dispose of Their E-Waste Properly; The Government Must Regulate E-Waste; The E-Waste Problem Is Greatly Exaggerated; Electronics Recycling Standards Often Fall Short; E-Waste Recycling Certification Will Help Stem the Illegal Waste Trade; Precious Metals from E-Waste Could Be Tomorrow's Jewelry"--Provided by publisher.
    Includes bibliographical references and index.
    ISBN 978-0-7377-5606-7 (hardback) -- ISBN 978-0-7377-5607-4 (paperback)
    1. Electronic waste--Juvenile literature. 2. Electronic apparatus and appliances--Environmental aspects--Juvenile literature. I. Thompson, Tamara.
    TD799.85.W435 2011
    363.72'88--dc23
                                                                            2011020386

Printed in the United States of America
    1 2 3 4 5   15 14 13 12 11

FD224

Contents

Introduction

The global demand for electronics has skyrocketed during the past two decades, and so has the problem of how to get rid of old, unwanted devices that typically contain toxic chemicals and heavy metals. According to the recycling industry, each year Americans throw out approximately 400 million electronic devices, making "e-waste"—discarded computers, TVs, cell phones, iPods, Kindles, DVD players, digital cameras, and myriad other consumer gizmos—the fastest growing waste stream, not just in the United States, but in the world. Such a high-tech heap might not be unavoidable, however; "planned obsolescence," according to some experts, unnecessarily increases the amount of electronic waste consumers generate many times over.

"Anyone who's had a cell phone fritz out after six months already knows all about planned obsolescence," says Ted Smith in a November 10, 2010, Examiner.com article. Smith is chair of the Electronics TakeBack Coalition, a national coalition of more than thirty environmental and public health organizations working to promote green design and responsible recycling in the electronics industry. Planned obsolescence is exactly what it sounds like: a deliberate plan to make something obsolete.

As Giles Slade explains in his book *Made to Break: Technology and Obsolescence in America*, there are lots of different ways to limit the lifespan of a product so that consumers will want or need to buy more of it (and so the company can make more money). Companies routinely do it by using parts that wear out quickly and that cannot be replaced; incrementally adopting new technologies that give each product model new features or a little better performance than the last; or even simply by changing the style and look of the product frequently so that older models seem dated and out of fashion to trend-conscious consumers. All of these techniques of planned obsolescence encourage consumers to get rid of their old electronic devices and replace them with new ones—often while the old ones are still working.

In the United States, for example, cell phones that are built to last five years are routinely discarded in eighteen months or less, giving mobile phones the shortest life cycle of any electronic device. North Americans threw out more than 100 million cell phones and some 315 million computers in 2004; about 90 percent of them were still functional.

The US States Environmental Protection Agency's (EPA) Office of Solid Waste estimates that in 2005, the United States alone generated 2.63 million tons of e-waste. More than 87 percent of that (2.3 million tons) ended up in landfills or incinerators, while only 12.5 percent was collected for recycling. The statistics were not much improved five years later: 85 percent and 15 percent, respectively, in 2010. The e-waste is piling up so fast that pretty soon there will not be enough space to store it, enough containers to hold it, or enough ships or trucks to transport it, according to some experts.

But those numbers do not just mean sky-high piles of cell phones, laptops, and other electronics that are largely still useable. Says Smith, "Most of our electronics are laden with problematic substances like lead, mercury, polyvinyl chloride and brominated flame retardants, so when they break it's not just a bummer, it's a global toxic issue." Properly recycling electronic components is essential in order to prevent the hazardous contamination of soil and water. Cell phones are especially problematic because they are too small to easily take apart for recycling, and it is easier and cheaper to simply dispose of them.

Because of high costs in the United States, even when they are collected for recycling most electronics are not taken apart here, but are instead illegally shipped overseas for unsafe dismantling. Because wages are low and there is little or no environmental regulation, developing countries such as China, India, and Senegal are especially vulnerable to toxic pollution, worker exploitation, and serious health hazards from unscrupulous electronic waste exports from the developed world. Many of the current legal efforts in America, Europe, and Asia seek to address this blatant example of environmental and social injustice.

In "The Story of Electronics," an eight-minute animated web film, environmental advocate Annie Leonard takes on the electronics industry's "design for the dump" mentality and urges companies to make less toxic, more easily recyclable, and longer-lasting products.

"If we can figure out how to make an iPhone remember where you parked your car," says Leonard in the November 10, 2010, Examiner.com article, "then we can figure out how to make electronics that aren't filled with toxic chemicals and en route to the trash can just months after we buy them." The core message of Leonard's popular film is: "Make 'em safe, make 'em last, and take 'em back."

Although there is broad agreement among environmentalists, governments, and the electronics industry that e-waste is a serious problem, there is much disagreement on the best way to handle it and, more to the point, who should pay for it.

The United States does not have a national e-waste policy, and although it signed the Basel Convention—an international treaty designed to reduce the movement of hazardous waste between nations, and specifically to prevent its transfer from developed to less developed countries—in 1989, it still has yet to ratify it. While European countries have made big strides in regulating e-waste, America has only a patchwork of state and local laws aimed at e-waste creation, handling, or export.

Leonard, for one, believes that laws requiring companies to take back and recycle or refurbish the products they manufacture are a step in the right direction, and that they could even spur economic competition. "With take-back laws and citizen action to demand greener products, we are starting a race to the top, where designers compete to make long-lasting, toxic-free products," says Leonard at the website for the Story of Stuff Project. While some electronics makers try desperately to protect their profit margins from the costs associated with e-waste, industry titans such as Nokia, Sony, Dell, Hewlett-Packard, and Apple realize that good environmental steward-ship is good business, and they are setting the standard for voluntarily reducing toxins and offering free take-back pro-grams for their products. Whether the rest of the electronics industry will follow suit without being forced to is unclear, however.

Despite the gains made by private business and govern-ments, e-waste activists still say the solution starts with edu-cating consumers so that they can vote with their dollars by buying environmentally responsible products and holding manufacturers responsible for the product's end-life. As Slade writes, "Now more than ever, end-users of new technology need to pursue higher levels of technological literacy in order to negotiate the complex interactions among technology, soci-ety and the environment. Ignorance of these interactions ef-fectively grants a permissions slip for technological hazards to persist."

Whether government regulation is the right solution or whether the pressure of educated consumers alone can force the private sector to take responsibility for the e-waste prob-lem remains to be seen. One thing, however, is certain: the outcome will have far-reaching implications for the environ-ment, e-waste workers, and consumers both today and for years to come. The authors in *At Issue: What Is The Impact of E- Waste?* represent a wide range of viewpoints in the debate over what should be done to reduce the footprint and toxicity of electronic waste and who should pay for it.

1

Electronic Waste: An Overview

United Nations University

Through its research initiatives, the United Nations University works to resolve the pressing global problems that concern the United Nations, its peoples, and its member states.

Global sales of electronic products are skyrocketing, and so is the problem of properly disposing of old or broken items. Electronics contain a variety of toxic metals, plastics, and chemicals, so properly recycling their components is essential to prevent contamination of the environment. Unfortunately, most electronics are not recycled properly and are instead illegally shipped overseas for unsafe dismantling. Because wages are low and there is very little environmental regulation, developing countries, such as China, India, and Senegal, are especially vulnerable to toxic pollution and worker exploitation from exporters of electronic waste, nearly all of which comes from the developed world. Training developing nations to responsibly handle e-waste would protect the health of workers and their families, safeguard the environment, and boost local economies.

Sales of electronic products in countries like China and India and across continents such as Africa and Latin America are set to rise sharply in the next 10 years.

And, unless action is stepped up to properly collect and recycle materials, many developing countries face the spectre of hazardous e-waste mountains with serious consequences for the environment and public health, according to UN

United Nations University, "Urgent Need to Prepare Developing Countries for Surge in E-Wastes," unu.edu, February 22, 2010. Reproduced by permission.

[United Nations] experts in a landmark report released today [February 22, 2010] by UNEP [United Nations Environment Programme].

Issued at a meeting of Basel Convention and other world chemical authorities prior to UNEP's Governing Council meeting in Bali, Indonesia, the report, "Recycling—from E-Waste to Resources," used data from 11 representative developing countries to estimate current and future e-waste generation—which includes old and dilapidated desk and laptop computers, printers, mobile phones, pagers, digital photo and music devices, refrigerators, toys and televisions.

In South Africa and China for example, the report predicts that by 2020 e-waste from old computers will have jumped by 200 to 400 percent from 2007 levels, and by 500% in India. By that same year in China, e-waste from discarded mobile phones will be about 7 times higher than 2007 levels and, in India, 18 times higher.

By 2020, e-waste from televisions will be 1.5 to 2 times higher in China and India while in India e-waste from discarded refrigerators will double or triple.

E-waste . . . includes old and dilapidated desk and laptop computers, printers, mobile phones, pagers, digital photo and music devices, refrigerators, toys and televisions.

China Faces Formidable Problems

China already produces about 2.3 million tonnes (2010 estimate) domestically, second only to the United States with about 3 million tonnes. And, despite having banned e-waste imports, China remains a major e-waste dumping ground for developed countries.

Moreover, most e-waste in China is improperly handled, much of it incinerated by backyard recyclers to recover valuable metals like gold—practices that release steady plumes of far-reaching toxic pollution and yield very low metal recovery rates compared to state-of-the-art industrial facilities.

"This report gives new urgency to establishing ambitious, formal and regulated processes for collecting and managing e-waste via the setting up of large, efficient facilities in China," says UN Under-Secretary-General Achim Steiner, Executive Director of UNEP. "China is not alone in facing a serious challenge. India, Brazil, Mexico and others may also face rising environmental damage and health problems if e-waste recycling is left to the vagaries of the informal sector.

"In addition to curbing health problems, boosting developing country e-waste recycling rates can have the potential to generate decent employment, cut greenhouse gas emissions and recover a wide range of valuable metals including silver, gold, palladium, copper and indium—by acting now and planning forward many countries can turn an e-challenge into an e-opportunity," he added.

The Report's Findings

The report was issued at the Simultaneous Extraordinary Meetings of the Conferences of the Parties to the Basel, Rotterdam and Stockholm Conventions on enhancing their cooperation and coordination (ExCOP).

It was co-authored by the Swiss EMPA, Umicore and United Nations University (UNU), part of the global think tank StEP (Solving the E-waste Problem), which includes UNEP and Basel Convention Secretariat among its 50+ members. Hosted by UNU in Bonn, Germany, the think tank convenes experts from industry, government, international organizations, NGOs [non-governmental organizations] and science. A grant from the European Commission, Directorate-General for the Environment, funded the report's preparation.

The report cites a variety of sources to illustrate growth of the e-waste problem:

- Global e-waste generation is growing by about 40 million tons a year

- Manufacturing mobile phones and personal computers consumes 3 per cent of the gold and silver mined worldwide each year; 13 per cent of the palladium and 15 percent of cobalt

- Modern electronics contain up to 60 different elements—many valuable, some hazardous, and some both

- Carbon dioxide emissions from the mining and production of copper and precious and rare metals used in electrical and electronic equipment are estimated at over 23 million tonnes—0.1 percent of global emissions (not including emissions linked to steel, nickel or aluminum, nor those linked to manufacturing the devices)

- In the US, more than 150 million mobiles and pagers were sold in 2008, up from 90 million five years before

- Globally, more than 1 billion mobile phones were sold in 2007, up from 896 million in 2006

- Countries like Senegal and Uganda can expect e-waste flows from PCs alone to increase 4 to 8-fold by 2020

Global e-waste generation is growing by about 40 million tons a year.

- Given the infrastructure expense and technology skills required to create proper facilities for efficient and environmentally sound metal recovery, the report suggests facilitating exports of critical e-scrap fractions like circuit boards or batteries from smaller countries to OECD-level, certified end-processors.

E-Waste Recycling Could Fuel Green Economy

Says Konrad Osterwalder, UN Under-Secretary General and Rector of UNU: "One person's waste can be another's raw material. The challenge of dealing with e-waste represents an important step in the transition to a green economy. This report outlines smart new technologies and mechanisms which, combined with national and international policies, can transform waste into assets, creating new businesses with decent green jobs. In the process, countries can help cut pollution linked with mining and manufacturing, and with the disposal of old devices."

The report assesses current policies, skills, waste collection networks and informal recycling in 11 developing economies in Asia, Africa and the Americas: China, India, South Africa, Uganda, Senegal, Kenya, Morocco, Brazil, Columbia, Mexico and Peru. It also outlines options for sustainable e-waste management in those countries.

The data includes equipment generated nationally but does not include waste imports, both legal and illegal, which are substantial in India, China and other emerging economies. Broken down by e-waste type, the report estimates e-waste generation today as follows:

- China: 500,000 tonnes from refrigerators, 1.3 million tonnes from TVs, 300,000 tonnes from personal computers

- India: over 100,000 tonnes from refrigerators, 275,000 tonnes from TVs, 56,300 tonnes from personal computers, 4,700 tonnes from printers and 1,700 tonnes from mobile phones

- Colombia: about 9,000 tonnes from refrigerators, over 18,000 tonnes from TVs, 6,500 tonnes from personal computers, 1,300 tonnes from printers, 1,200 tonnes from mobile phones

- Kenya: about 9,000 tonnes from refrigerators, over 18,000 tonnes from TVs, 6,500 tonnes from personal computers, 1,300 tonnes from printers, 1,200 tonnes from mobile phones

The report also includes data on per capita sales of electrical and electronic goods. For example South Africa and Mexico lead in personal computer sales with the equivalent of 24 sold per 1,000 people. Brazil, Mexico and Senegal generate more e-waste per capita from personal computers than the other countries surveyed.

Finding the Way Forward

Developing vibrant national recycling schemes is complex and simply financing and transferring high tech equipment from developed countries is unlikely to work, according to the report.

It says China's lack of a comprehensive e-waste collection network, combined with competition from the lower-cost informal sector, has held back state-of-the art e-waste recycling plants.

It also notes a successful pilot in Bangalore, India, to transform the operations of informal e-waste collection and management.

Brazil, Colombia, Mexico, Morocco and South Africa are cited as places with great potential to introduce state of the art e-waste recycling technologies because the informal e-waste sector is relatively small.

Kenya, Peru, Senegal and Uganda are said to have relatively low e-waste volumes today, but these are likely to grow. All four would benefit from capacity building in so-called pre-processing technologies such as manual dismantling of e-waste.

The report recommends countries establish e-waste management centers of excellence, building on existing organizations working in the area of recycling and waste management.

Existing bodies include those supported by the United Nations including the more than 40 National Cleaner Production Centers established by the UN Industrial and Development Organization and the regional centers established under the Basel Convention on the Control of Transboundary Movements of Hazardous Wastes and their Disposal.

2

Planned Obsolescence Creates Unnecessary E-Waste

Giles Slade

Giles Slade is a writer whose book, Made to Break: Technology and Obsolescence in America, *won the International Publisher's Gold Medal for best environmental book of 2007.*

One of the main reasons there is so much electronic waste in the world is that manufacturers design products for deliberate obsolescence—that is, they design them to become obsolete in one way or another so that consumers will need to replace them with new ones, and thus the manufacturers sell more goods. A product can become obsolete because it does not last very long and it breaks, or because a new model is introduced with features that are incompatible with the old one, or even because the product gets a new color or style that consumers are convinced they desire. While this type of marketing strategy is highly profitable for companies, it is bad for consumers and even worse for the planet. If things keep going as they are, there will not even be enough shipping containers in the world to hold and transport both the new electronic goods and all of the e-waste the old goods generate. Global businesses must be responsible and stop putting profits before the planet by reducing the waste footprint of the products they create.

For no better reason than that a century of advertising has conditioned us to want more, better, and faster from any consumer good we purchase, in 2004 about 315 million working PCs were retired in North America. Of these, as many as 10 percent would be refurbished and reused, but most would go straight to the trash heap. These still-functioning but obsolete computers represented an enormous increase over the 63 million working PCs dumped into American landfills in 2003. In 1997, although a PC monitor lasted six or seven years, a CPU was expected to last only four or five. By 2003 informed consumers expected only two years of use from the new systems they were purchasing, and today the life expectancy of most PCs is even less.

In 2005 more than 100 million cell phones were discarded in the United States. This 50,000 tons of still-usable equipment joined another 200,000 tons of cell phones already awaiting dismantling and disposal. Unlike PCs, the compact design of cell phones resists disassembly for recycling—it's much easier just to throw phones away and make new ones. So despite the fact that they weigh only a fraction of what PCs weigh, discarded cell phones represent a toxic time bomb waiting to enter America's landfills and water table.

Obsolete Electronics

Cell phones and PCs travel in the company of a vast assortment of obsolete IT electronics, including last year's Palms, Blackberries, Notebooks, printers, copiers, monitors, scanners, modems, hubs, docking ports, digital cameras, LCD projectors, Zip drives, speakers, keyboards, mice, GameBoys, Walkmen, CD players, VCRs, and DVD players—all awaiting disposal. PlayStations, Xboxes, and iPods are not far behind. Obsolete cathode ray tubes [CRT] used in computer monitors will already be in the trash (superseded by LCDs, as in Japan) by the time a U.S. government mandate goes into effect in 2009 committing all of the country to High-Definition [HD] TV. The CRTs of analog televisions are constructed along the same general design as those of PC monitors, but they are larger—often *much* larger—and are made up of about 55 percent toxic lead glass, while a monitor is only about 28 to 36 percent. But the looming problem is not just the oversized analog TV sitting in the family room, which will require a team of professional movers to haul away. The fact is that no one really knows how many smaller analog TVs still lurk in basements, attics, garages, and kitchens, not to mention the back rooms of sports bars, fitness clubs, and other commercial sites.

What *is* known is frightening. Since the 1970s, TV sales have achieved about a 95 percent penetration rate in American homes, compared to the 50 percent penetration rate computers achieved in the 1990s. For more than a decade, about 20 to 25 million TVs have been sold annually in the United States, while only 20,000 are recycled each year. So as federal regulations mandating HDTV come into effect in 2009, an unknown but substantially larger number of analog TVs will join the hundreds of millions of computer monitors entering America's overcrowded, pre-toxic waste stream. Just this one-time disposal of "brown goods" will, alone, more than double the hazardous waste problem in North America.

The e-waste problem will soon reach such gigantic proportions that it will overwhelm our shipping capacity.

Running Out of Room

Meanwhile, no one has figured out what to do with plain old telephone service receivers, whose lead-solder connections and PVC cases are quickly becoming obsolete as consumers make the switch to 3G cell phones and VoI (voice over the Internet). As these archaic devices are piled on top of other remnants of wired technology, America's landfills—already overflowing—will reach a point where they can no longer offer a suitable burial for the nation's electronic junk.

Until recently the United States shipped much of its toxic e-waste to China, India, Pakistan, Bangladesh, and other economically desperate countries in the developing world. But exportation is, at best, a stop-gap strategy. Following the Basel Convention, the United Nations slowed electronic waste shipments to these ports. But more practically, the e-waste problem will soon reach such gigantic proportions that it will overwhelm our shipping capacity. The world simply cannot produce enough *containers* for America to continue at its current level as an exporter of both electronic goods and electronic waste. Consequently, all of these discarded and highly toxic components represent an insurmountable future storage problem. We do not have enough time, money, or space in the continental United States to create enough landfills to store and then ignore America's growing pile of electronic trash.

What brought us to this pass?

Deliberate obsolescence in all its forms—technological, psychological, or planned—is a uniquely American invention.

Deliberate Obsolescence

Deliberate obsolescence in all its forms—technological, psychological, or planned—is a uniquely American invention. Not only did we invent disposable products, ranging from diapers to cameras to contact lenses, but we invented the very concept of disposability itself, as a necessary precursor to our rejection of tradition and our promotion of progress and change. As American manufacturers learned how to exploit obsolescence, American consumers increasingly accepted it in every aspect of their lives. Actual use of the word "obsolescence" to describe out-of-date consumer products began to show up in the early twentieth century when modern household appliances replaced older stoves and fireplaces, and steel pots replaced iron ones. But it was the electric starter in automobiles, introduced in 1913, that raised obsolescence to national prominence by rendering all previous cars obsolete. Even the most modern American women hated hand-cranking their cars and were greatly relieved when they could simply push a start button on a newer model. The earliest phase of product obsolescence, then, is called *technological obsolescence,* or obsolescence due to technological innovation.

The second stage of product obsolescence occurred about a decade later, in 1923. Executives who had migrated to General Motors from the chemical and dye-making giant DuPont adapted a marketing strategy from what was then America's third largest and most rapidly growing industry: textiles and fashions. Instead of waiting for technological innovations that would push consumers to trade in their older-model cars, General Motors [GM] turned to sleek styling as a way of making newer cars more desirable and pulling potential buyers into the showroom. The success of GM's cosmetic changes to the 1923 Chevrolet indicated that consumers were willing to trade up for style, not just for technological improvements, long before their old cars wore out. This strategy was so successful that it spread quickly to many other American industries, such as watches and radios. The annual model change adopted by carmakers is an example of *psychological, progressive,* or *dynamic obsolescence.* All of these terms refer to the mechanism of changing product style as a way to manipulate consumers into repetitive buying.

Manipulating Failure

The most recent stage in the history of product obsolescence began when producers recognized their ability to manipulate the failure rate of manufactured materials. After prolonged use, any product will fail because its materials become worn or stressed. This is normal. But during the [Great] Depression, manufacturers were forced to return to the practice of adulteration—the nineteenth-century technique of using inferior materials in manufactured goods—as a simple cost-cutting measure: inferior materials lowered unit costs. But these same manufacturers soon realized that adulteration also stimulated demand. After a decade of unprecedented affluence and consumption during the 1920s, consumer demand fell radically with the onset of the Depression, and in desperation manufacturers used inferior materials to deliberately shorten the life spans of products and force consumers to purchase replacements.

Planned obsolescence is the catch-all phrase used to describe the assortment of techniques used to artificially limit the durability of a manufactured good in order to stimulate repetitive consumption. To achieve shorter product lives and sell more goods, manufacturers in the 1930s began to base their choice of materials on scientific tests by newly formed research and development departments. These tests determined when each of the product's specific components would fail. One of the few known examples of this monopolistic (and hence illegal) strategy was a change, proposed but never implemented, to shorten the life of General Electric's flashlight bulbs in order to increase demand by as much as 60 percent.

Planned obsolescence is the catch-all phrase used to describe the assortment of techniques used to artificially limit the durability of a manufactured good in order to stimulate repetitive consumption.

As obsolescence became an increasingly useful manufacturing and marketing tool, an eclectic assortment of advertisers, bankers, business analysts, communications theorists, economists, engineers, industrial designers, and even real estate brokers contrived ways to describe, control, promote, and exploit the market demand that obsolescence created. What these approaches had in common was their focus on a radical break with tradition in order to deliver products, and prosperity, to the greatest number of people—and in the process to gain market share and make a buck. Both goals strike us today as quintessentially American in spirit.

Comment on Culture

But even as these professionals were inventing the means to exploit obsolescence, a number of articulate American critics began to see this manipulation of the public as the very epitome of what was wrong with our culture and its economic system. The former journalist Vance Packard raised the issue powerfully in his debut book, *The Hidden Persuaders*, in 1957, which revealed how advertisers relied on motivational research to manipulate potential buyers. Others, including Norman Cousins, John Kenneth Galbraith, Marshall McLuhan, Archibald MacLeish, and Victor Papanek, would follow Packard's lead in pointing out how the media create artificial needs within vulnerable consumers. The sheer volume of print Americans have devoted to this topic since 1927 demonstrates that obsolescence has become a touchstone of the American consciousness. . . .

A few years back, as I was visiting a touring exhibit called "Eternal Egypt" with my ten-year-old son, it occurred to me that while the ancient Egyptians built great monuments to endure for countless generations, just about everything we produce in North America is made to break. If human history reserves a privileged place for the Egyptians because of their rich conception of the afterlife, what place will it reserve for a people who, in their seeming worship of convenience and greed, left behind mountains of electronic debris? What can be said of a culture whose legacies to the future are mounds of hazardous materials and a poisoned water supply? Will America's pyramids be pyramids of waste?

3

Developing Countries Are a Dumping Ground for Hazardous E-Waste

Matt Ford

Matt Ford is a freelance journalist based in England. His work has appeared in The Independent, The Guardian, *and* The Daily Telegraph, *and he writes regularly for CNN.com.*

At e-waste dump sites in such countries as Nigeria and Ghana, the ground and water are contaminated with a variety of toxic substances, such as lead, cadmium, phthalates, and dioxins, that come from improperly dismantled electronic equipment. Such conditions are the rule rather than the exception in developing countries that process e-waste. Experts estimate that a stunning 80 percent of the global e-waste generated each year (20 to 50 million tons) is not recycled properly. The US and European countries are the primary exporters of e-waste to the developing world, and much of it is shipped there illegally. The developed world must take a strong stand to stop the spread of e-waste, and developing countries must establish environmentally sound recycling practices and learn to capitalize on the influx of equipment by refurbishing and reusing electronics for their own technology needs.

Clouds of black smoke from burning plastic hang over the sites of Nigeria's vast dumps, as tiny figures pick their way through slicks of oily water, past cracked PC monitors and television screens.

Matt Ford, "Sifting Through the Mounting Problem of E-Waste," CNN.com, August 10, 2009. Courtesy CNN. Reproduced by permission.

But it isn't just a cut from broken glass these mainly young scavengers are risking. Much of the discarded electronic kit contains tiny—but valuable—quantities of aluminum, copper, cadmium and other minerals, all of which can be sold on, if they can be recovered.

However they also contain highly toxic materials, which have been linked to reproductive problems and cancers.

"People living and working on and around the dump sites, many of whom are children, are exposed to a cocktail of dangerous chemicals that can cause severe damage to health, including cancer, damage to the nervous system and to brain development in children," Kim Schoppink, Toxics Campaigner at Greenpeace, told CNN.

"The open burning creates even more hazardous chemicals among which are cancerous dioxins."

No studies have been done on the extent of the chemical pollution of such sites in Nigeria, but in 2008 a Greenpeace report on similar dumps in nearby Ghana confirmed that high levels of lead, phthalates and dioxins were present in soils and the water of a nearby lagoon.

A Chinese academic report published in "Environmental Health Perspectives" in 2007 confirmed that children living in the same area had higher levels of toxic metals in their blood than other children living nearby.

According to the United Nations Environment Program around 20 to 50 million tons of e-waste are generated worldwide each year.

Shipped from the West

There is increasing evidence that this new health and environment problem is arriving in shipping containers from Western countries. Nigeria is one of the principal global destinations for "e-waste"—the catch-all term for discarded consumer electronics.

Some of this may have been legitimately handed in to be recycled in an EU [European Union] or U.S. city, but lax enforcement, vague legislation and a lack of political will has meant that it instead passes through a network of traders keen to profit from developing countries' hunger for hi-tech and a burgeoning second hand market.

According to the United Nations Environment Program around 20 to 50 million tons of e-waste are generated worldwide each year.

In 2008 a Greenpeace study, "Not in My Backyard", found that in Europe only 25 percent of the e-waste was recycled safety. In the U.S. it is only 20 percent and in developing countries it is less than one percent.

Extrapolating out from these figures the report concluded that a massive 80 percent of e-waste generated worldwide is not properly recycled. Some is burnt in Western incinerators or buried in landfill sites.

A massive 80 percent of e-waste generated worldwide is not properly recycled.

But much is exported to developing countries including India, China, Pakistan, Nigeria and Ghana. When it arrives, a further percentage may be repaired and sold on to populations desperate for affordable technology. But anything beyond the skills of local traders will end up dumped.

It's a profitable business, and is already attracting the attention of organized crime. A report issued by the United Nations in July [2009] said that the criminal gangs behind much of the drug trade in West Africa were becoming involved with e-waste trading.

The volume of material on the move is staggering. In 2005, more than 500 containers full of e-waste entered Nigerian ports every month, according to the Basel Action Network, a U.S. NGO [non-governmental organization] campaigning on issues surrounding toxic waste.

Each one contains 10 to 15 tons of e-waste, totaling 80,000 to 90,000 tons per year. These figures are likely to have increased in recent years.

There seems little doubt that much of this waste is finding its way to Africa from Western countries. The Basel Action Network and Dutch NGO Danwatch have traced equipment from Europe to Nigerian dumps and earlier this year Greenpeace placed a radio tracking device in a broken TV handed in for safe recycling in the UK, but followed it to a Nigerian market.

"Greenpeace is disappointed especially by U.S. and EU authorities," said Schoppink.

"It is toxic waste from the U.S. and EU countries that is causing serious environmental and health problems in Nigeria, a country without the means to deal with this problem.

"The U.S. and EU must play the biggest role in stopping the spread of e-waste; they are most responsible for the problem and have the resources to tackle it. The export of e-waste from the EU is illegal under the Basel Convention and the Waste Shipment Directive, but the laws are not being sufficiently implemented. In the U.S., there is no such law banning this practice.

"In Nigeria the government is talking about stopping imports, but there has been no progress on this to date."

Signs of Progress

There are calls from environmental groups like Greenpeace for electronics producers to do more to phase out their use of hazardous substances, and there are some signs of progress.

Several electronics companies already make products using fewer hazardous substances, and others, including Nokia, Philips and Samsung, are setting up voluntary collection and recycling systems in countries where they are not legally obliged to. Apple claims its products are now almost entirely free of the worst toxic chemicals.

"If producers continue to use hazardous chemicals in their electronics and to fail to take responsibility for the safe disposal of their products, e-waste will continue to be dumped in developing countries," said Schoppink.

"The pollution and related health problems in countries where e-waste is dumped will increase massively as the amount of electronics used worldwide is growing exponentially and the number of countries used as dump sites will grow."

Closing the Digital Divide

But while the developing world needs the U.S. and EU to take responsibility for their waste, it also needs their discarded computers to train and build a 21st century workforce.

"Nobody is arguing that Africa should be denied access to computers," said Tony Roberts, Founder and Chief Executive Officer of Computer Aid International, a charity licensed by the UK Environment Agency, which provides recycled computers to developing countries to improve education and healthcare.

"Technical colleges and universities are always short of resources. It is, of course, essential to developing economies escaping poverty to have access to affordable modern technology."

Computer Aid works to close the digital divide between the north and southern hemispheres and offers corporations, including Coca Cola, as well as individuals, a positive way of disposing of electronics. They also believe learning about responsibility for that technology is a crucial part of the exchange.

"Computer Aid argues that, in addition to the PCs, it is essential to also build the skills, knowledge and operating capacity in every country to manage responsible re-use programs and environmentally sound end-of-life recycling."

In the end, this is about everyone involved—particularly the developed nations—taking responsibility for their waste.

"It is clear that companies have a moral obligation to treat Africa in exactly the same way that they do, say, Germany," said Roberts. Until then, toxic black smoke will continue to cast a shadow over lives across the developing world.

4

Illegal E-Waste from America Poisons Communities Overseas

CBS News

CBS News's 60 Minutes *is an investigative news magazine that has aired weekly on the broadcast network since 1968.*

The 60 Minutes *news program visited an electronics recycling center in Denver and followed some of the e-waste collected there to see where it would be processed. Despite assurances from the recycling company that it always follows good practices, the e-waste was put on a cargo ship, where* 60 Minutes *tracked it to a port in Hong Kong. Because the shipment was illegal, authorities there rejected it. If they hadn't, it likely would have ended up in a town like Guiyu, China, where workers unsafely take apart machines to extract valuable metals and other components. Communities like Guiyu are poisoned by the toxic substances that come from e-waste shipped from America, and local politicians and gangsters keep close control of the facilities so that outsiders do not see what is taking place there. This story demonstrates that even so-called reputable e-waste recyclers cut corners and are out to make a buck wherever they can by cheaply exporting e-waste to developing countries, instead of spending more money to properly dismantle it here in the United States.*

CBS News, "Following the Trail of Toxic E-Waste. *60 Minutes* Follows America's Toxic Electronic Waste as It Is Illegally Shipped to Become China's Dirty Secret," CBSnews .com, August 30, 2009. Reproduced by permission of CBS News Archives.

60 Minutes is going to take you to one of the most toxic places on Earth—a place that government officials and gangsters don't want you to see. It's a town in China where you can't breathe the air or drink the water, a town where the blood of the children is laced with lead. It's worth risking a visit because, as correspondent Scott Pelley first reported last November [2008] much of the poison is coming out of the homes, schools and offices of America.

This is a story about recycling—about how your best intentions to be green can be channeled into an underground sewer that flows from the United States and into the wasteland.

That wasteland is piled with the burning remains of some of the most expensive, sophisticated stuff that consumers crave. And *60 Minutes* and correspondent Scott Pelley discovered that the gangs who run this place wanted to keep it a secret.

What are they hiding? The answer lies in the first law of the digital age: newer is better. In with the next thing, and out with the old TV, phone or computer. All of this becomes obsolete, electronic garbage called "e-waste."

Computers may seem like sleek, high-tech marvels. But what's inside them?

"Lead, cadmium, mercury, chromium, polyvinyl chlorides. All of these materials have known toxicological effects that range from brain damage to kidney disease to mutations, cancers," Allen Hershkowitz, a senior scientist and authority on waste management at the Natural Resources Defense Council, explained.

"The problem with e-waste is that it is the fastest-growing component of the municipal waste stream worldwide," he said.

Asked what he meant by "fastest-growing," Hershkowitz said, "Well, we throw out about 130,000 computers every day in the United States."

And he said over 100 million cell phones are thrown out annually.

The problem with e-waste is that it is the fastest-growing component of the municipal waste stream worldwide.

Recycling Event Is the Beginning

At a recycling event in Denver, *60 Minutes* found cars bumper-to-bumper for blocks, in a line that lasted for hours. They were there to drop off their computers, PDAs, TVs and other electronic waste.

Asked what he thought happens once his e-waste goes into recycling, one man told Pelley, "Well my assumption is they break it apart and take all the heavy metals out and then try to recycle some of the stuff that's bad."

Most folks in line were hoping to do the right thing, expecting that their waste would be recycled in state-of-the-art facilities that exist here in America. But really, there's no way for them to know where all of this is going. The recycling industry is exploding and, as it turns out, some so-called recyclers are shipping the waste overseas, where it's broken down for the precious metals inside.

Executive Recycling, of Englewood, Colo., which ran the Denver event, promised the public on its Web site: "Your e-waste is recycled properly, right here in the U.S.—not simply dumped on somebody else."

That policy helped Brandon Richter, the CEO of Executive Recycling, win a contract with the city of Denver and expand operations into three western states.

Asked what the problem is with shipping this waste overseas, Richter told Pelley, "Well, you know, they've got low-income labor over there. So obviously they don't have all of the right materials, the safety equipment to handle some of this material."

Where It Ended Up

Executive does recycling in-house, but *60 Minutes* was curious about shipping containers that were leaving its Colorado yard. *60 Minutes* found one container filled with monitors. They're especially hazardous because each picture tube, called a cathode ray tube or CRT, contains several pounds of lead. It's against U.S. law to ship them overseas without special permission. *60 Minutes* took down the container's number and followed it to Tacoma, Wash., where it was loaded on a ship.

The container that started in Denver was just one of thousands of containers on an underground, often illegal smuggling route, taking America's trash to the Far East.

When the container left Tacoma, *60 Minutes* followed it for 7,459 miles to Victoria Harbor, Hong Kong.

It turns out the container that started in Denver was just one of thousands of containers on an underground, often illegal smuggling route, taking America's electronic trash to the Far East.

Our guide to that route was Jim Puckett, founder of the Basel Action Network, a watchdog group named for the treaty that is supposed to stop rich countries from dumping toxic waste on poor ones. Puckett runs a program to certify ethical recyclers. And he showed *60 Minutes* what's piling up in Hong Kong.

"It's literally acres of computer monitors," Pelley commented. "Is it legal to import all of these computer monitors into Hong Kong?"

"No way. It is absolutely illegal, both from the standpoint of Hong Kong law but also U.S. law and Chinese law. But it's happening," Puckett said.

60 Minutes followed the trail to a place Puckett discovered in southern China—a sort of Chernobyl of electronic waste—

the town of Guiyu. But we weren't there very long before we were picked up by the cops and taken to City Hall. We told the mayor we wanted to see recycling.

So he personally drove us to a shop.

Officials Do Not Want Publicity

"Let me explain what's happening here," Pelley remarked while in Guiyu. "We were brought into the mayor's office. The mayor told us that we're essentially not welcome here, but he would show us one place where computers are being dismantled and this is that place. A pretty tidy shop. The mayor told us that we would be welcome to see the rest of the town, but that the town wouldn't be prepared for our visit for another year.

"So we were allowed to shoot at that location for about five minutes," Pelley explained further. "And we're back in the mayor's car headed back to City Hall, where I suspect we'll be given another cup of tea and sent on our way out of town with a police escort no doubt."

And we were. But the next day, in a different car and on a different road, we got in.

"This is really the dirty little secret of the electronic age," Jim Puckett said.

Greenpeace has been filming around Guiyu and caught the recycling work. Women were heating circuit boards over a coal fire, pulling out chips and pouring off the lead solder. Men were using what is literally a medieval acid recipe to extract gold. Pollution has ruined the town. Drinking water is trucked in. Scientists have studied the area and discovered that Guiyu has the highest levels of cancer-causing dioxins in the world. They found pregnancies are six times more likely to end in miscarriage, and that seven out of ten kids have too much lead in their blood.

"These people are not just working with these materials, they're living with them. They're all around their homes," Pelley told Allen Hershkowitz.

"The situation in Guiyu is actually pre-capitalist. It's mercantile. It reverts back to a time when people lived where they worked, lived at their shop. Open, uncontrolled burning of plastics. Chlorinated and brominated plastics is known worldwide to cause the emission of polychlorinated and polybrominated dioxins. These are among the most toxic compounds known on earth," Hershkowitz explained.

"We have a situation where we have 21st century toxics being managed in a 17th century environment."

We have a situation where we have 21st century toxics being managed in a 17th century environment.

'Desperate People Do Desperate Things'

The recyclers are peasant farmers who couldn't make a living on the land. Destitute, they've come by the thousands to get $8 a day. Greenpeace introduced us to some of them. They were afraid and didn't want to be seen, but theirs are the hands that are breaking down America's computers.

"The air I breathe in every day is so pungent I can definitely feel it in my windpipe and affecting my lungs. It makes me cough all the time," one worker told Pelley, with the help of a translator.

"If you're worried about your lungs and you're burning your hands, do you ever think about giving this up?" Pelley asked.

"Yes, I have thought of it," the worker said.

Asked why he doesn't give it up, the worker told him, "Because the money's good."

"You know, it struck me, talking to those workers the other day, that they were destitute and they're happy to have this work," Pelley told Puckett.

"Well, desperate people will do desperate things," Puckett replied. "But we should never put them in that situation. You know, it's a hell of a choice between poverty and poison. We should never make people make that choice."

Pelley, Puckett, and the *60 Minutes* team passed by a riverbed that had been blackened by the ash of burned e-waste.

"Oh, man, this is—it's unbelievably acrid and choking," Pelley said, coughing.

It's a hell of a choice between poverty and poison. We should never make people make that choice.

"This is an ash river. This is detritus from burning all this material and this is what the kids get to play in," Puckett explained.

After a few minutes in the real recycling area, we were jumped.

Several men struggled for our cameras. The mayor hadn't wanted us to see this place, and neither did the businessmen who were profiting from it. They got a soil sample that we'd taken for testing, but we managed to wrestle the cameras back.

What were they afraid of?

"They're afraid of being found out," Puckett said. "This is smuggling. This is illegal. A lot of people are turning a blind eye here. And if somebody makes enough noise, they're afraid this is all gonna dry up."

Confronting the Source

Back in Denver, there's no threat of it drying up. In fact, it was a flood.

And Brandon Richter, CEO of Executive Recycling, was still warning of the dangers of shipping waste to China. "I just heard actually a child actually died over there breaking this material down, just getting all these toxins," he said.

Then Pelley told him we'd tracked his container to Hong Kong.

"This is a photograph from your yard, the Executive Recycling yard," Pelley told Richter, showing him a photo we'd taken of a shipping container in his yard. "We followed this container to Hong Kong."

"Okay," Richter replied.

"And I wonder why that would be?" Pelley asked.

"Hmm. I have no clue," Richter said.

"The Hong Kong customs people opened the container . . . and found it full of CRT screens which, as you probably know, is illegal to export to Hong Kong," Pelley said.

"Yeah, yep," Richter replied. "I don't know if that container was filled with glass. I doubt it was. We don't fill glass, CRT glass in those containers."

"This container was in your yard, filled with CRT screens, and exported to Hong Kong, which probably wouldn't be legal," Pelley said.

"No, absolutely not. Yeah," Richter said.

"Can you explain that?" Pelley asked.

"Yeah, it's not—it was not filled in our facility," Richter said.

Officials Investigate Further

But that's where *60 Minutes* filmed it. And we weren't the only ones asking questions. It turns out Hong Kong customs intercepted the container and sent it back to Executive Recycling, Englewood, Colorado, the contents listed as "waste: cathode ray tubes."

U.S. customs x-rayed the container and found the same thing. *60 Minutes* showed Richter this evidence, and later his lawyer told us the CRTs were exported under Executive Recycling's name, but without the company's permission.

"I know this is your job," Richter told Pelley. "But, unfortunately, you know, when you attack small business owners like this and you don't have all your facts straight, it's unfortunate, you know?"

But here's one more fact: the federal Government Accountability Office set up a sting in which U.S. investigators posed as foreign importers. Executive Recycling offered to sell 1,500 CRT computer monitors and 1,200 CRT televisions to the GAO's fictitious broker in Hong Kong. But Executive Recycling was not alone. The GAO report found that another 42 American companies were willing to do the same.

NOTE: *Since* 60 Minutes *first broadcast this story, federal agents executed a search warrant at the Executive Recycling headquarters as part of an ongoing investigation.*

5

Cell Phones Create Especially Problematic E-Waste

Earthworks

Earthworks is an environmental nonprofit organization that runs the grassroots "Recycle My Cell Phone" program to refurbish or recycle old cell phones nationwide.

Because cell phones are so small and cheap to manufacture, it is easier and less costly to just discard old ones and make new ones than it is to responsibly recycle or refurbish old phones. Because of this, mobile phones are one of the most ubiquitous types of e-waste in the world. Each year, some 130 million cell phones are discarded, and most of them end up in landfills where they leak such toxics as lead, mercury and arsenic into the soil and water. The nation's cell phone companies fail miserably when it comes to being responsible stewards for their products. The wireless industry must do more to educate consumers and its own personnel about the importance of properly recycling cell phones, and it must offer opportunities to do so. A company's responsibility does not end by setting up a used phone take-back program, however; they must go a step further to ensure that the collection and processing of the phones is done in an environmentally responsible way and that e-waste is not dumped or improperly handled after it is collected.

The wireless industry fails miserably when it comes to dealing with their cell phone e-waste. Most wireless devices can be re-used or recycled at a profit—but at least 98 percent

Earthworks, "Cell Phone Recycling Report Card," www.recyclemyphone.org, 2006. Reproduced by permission.

of all retired cell phones are not. Too often cell phones that are collected are not handled properly, and many end up "dumped" in developing countries where environmental safeguards are weak or non-existent. The *Recycle My Cell Phone* campaign is calling on the wireless industry to reverse this dangerous trend and commit to responsibly dealing with their e-waste problem.

The refurbishing and recycling of cell phones can have significant environmental and social consequences. The four primary wireless service providers (Cingular, Sprint, T-Mobile, and Verizon Wireless) that control 86 percent of the wireless market in the United States and the trade association that represents them have failed to adequately address this problem. It is worth noting, however, that Verizon Wireless, while it still has a long way to go, has made greater progress and did score higher than other providers in some areas. Three of four industry leaders have partnered with a recycling and refurbishing company—ReCellular—the only company that has been removed from the Electronic Recyclers Pledge of True Stewardship. Cingular, the other industry leader, partners with Hobi International—which has never been a Pledge signatory.

ReCellular's name was removed from the Pledge by mutual agreement after extensive negotiations with Pledge managers. The Pledge is the most rigorous criteria for sustainable and socially just electronics recycling.

Wireless service providers' failure to adequately promote cell phone recycling to their customers compounds the problem. A review of four major wireless providers indicates that, although considerable time and effort has been invested into developing take-back programs, they are generally ineffective. Making dozens of store visits, placing numerous phones calls to customer service representatives, searching the websites of all the companies reviewed, and surveying wireless customers across the country, our researchers found that accurate information on how to recycle cell phones is extremely difficult to obtain.

A Look at the Statistics

- 84 percent of surveyed consumers do not know if their wireless provider offers a recycling program.

- 70 percent of stores visited did not have visible drop-offs or promotional materials.

- Retail store employees across the board had trouble providing accurate information on their company's program.

- Less than 50 percent of telephone representatives provided accurate information on recycling.

- Not a single company's website prominently featured information about their recycling programs or links to these programs from their front page.

- None of the carriers sells phones labeled with a recycling symbol, and information on recycling is rarely provided inside the packaging of newly purchased phones.

- There is no evidence of any company promoting recycling in print, radio, or television placements on a national level, or in billing statements or text messages.

- Most importantly, companies cannot verify that the phones that are collected are being handled using the best environmental practices and social standards.

The U.S. Environmental Protection Agency (EPA) estimates that 130 million cell phones are discarded each year. When dismantled, their internal metal components translate into 65,000 tons of waste containing lead, cadmium, arsenic, beryllium, mercury and other toxic heavy metals and carcinogens. Tens of millions of old phones end up in landfills or incinerators annually, where toxics can find their way into our drinking water and air.

E-Waste Can Affect Human Health. E-waste can pollute drinking water, cause birth defects, and has been shown to create cancer clusters among workers handling it. The comprehensive health impacts of the mixtures and material combinations in the products are often not known.

Tens of millions of old phones end up in landfills or incinerators annually, where toxics can find their way into our drinking water and air.

E-Waste Is Often "Dumped" Because It's the Easier Thing to Do. Processing e-waste is a complicated, multi-step process. Developing countries often end up as the recipients of this waste due to cheap labor and weak regulatory climates. This "dumping" from wealthy nations shifts the burden of e-waste and the ecological and health hazards to nations ill-equipped to handle the problem.

Mismanagement of E-Waste Depletes Irreplaceable Natural Resources. The 130 million cell phones discarded each year contain almost $100 million worth of gold—the annual output of a medium-sized mine. Recycling these metals would prevent the creation of more than 14 million tons of mine waste.

In the production phase, massive open pit gold mines often use cyanide to extract gold and other metals. Mining is the single largest toxic polluter in the United States. Even before a new cell phone is purchased, at least 220 pounds of mine waste have already been generated to source the gold in the circuit board alone. After 18 months (the average cell phone lifespan), the device is tossed into a drawer, or worse, the trash.

This mismanagement fuels the demand for mining development in places it does not belong. New mines threaten rivers that supply drinking water to local communities and to fisheries that provide food and jobs. Valuable metals could instead be mined from discarded cell phones and other electronics.

If all the discarded cell phones in a single year were recycled, $150 million of metals would be recovered:

- 182,000 oz [ounces] of gold worth $100.5 million

- 1.9 million oz of silver worth $18.6 million

- 65,000 oz of palladium worth $18.5 million

- 5 million lbs of copper worth $10.9 million

If all the discarded cell phones in a single year were recycled, $150 million of metals would be recovered.

America Lacks an E-Waste Policy

Despite the growing pile of cell phone e-waste, there is currently no federal regulation of cell phone recycling in the United States. The U.S. Environmental Protection Agency has disregarded commissioned research that recommended cell phones be classified as hazardous waste, and their voluntary guidelines on cell phone recycling are inadequate in dealing with the scope of the problem.

Through the Cellular Telephone & Internet Association (CTIA), the wireless industry lobbies vigorously to convince consumers and decision-makers to accept "voluntary" e-waste programs, stifling state and national efforts to address the problem. States such as Maine, Massachusetts and Minnesota have attempted to address the issue on the state level but have faced serious challenges from industry interests. Only one state, California, has succeeded in passing legislation that requires "no cost" take-back within the state.

While attempting to evade responsibility in the U.S., the wireless industry complies with higher standards mandated in

Europe. In 2003 the European Union (EU) established the Waste and Electronic Equipment Directive which establishes collection, recycling and recovery targets for all types of electronic goods. It also requires corporations to take back their products free of charge. The EU is also working to eliminate the use of toxic substances such as lead, mercury and cadmium in electronic equipment and has issued a directive prohibiting their presence in newly manufactured products.

The Basel Convention was designed to prevent the generation of toxic wastes, such as cell phones, through the promotion of cleaner technologies, ensuring country self-sufficiency in managing their wastes, and most importantly, to stop the environmentally unjust practice of dumping hazardous wastes by developed countries to less developed countries.

168 countries are parties to the Basel Convention, and the United States is the only developed nation that has not ratified this Convention.

Consumers Want a Real Solution

EARTHWORKS research indicates that the vast majority of consumers are in the dark when it comes to cell phone recycling. According to our informal survey of 1,046 wireless customers, 84 percent of respondents were not aware if their service provider offered a take-back program for old cell phones. While they are bombarded with messages to buy, upgrade and expand their service contracts, consumers are rarely given information on how to recycle.

- 72 percent of consumers surveyed by EARTHWORKS are "dissatisfied" with the wireless industry's take-back efforts;

- 85 percent described themselves as "very concerned" with the manner in which their phones were recycled.

Annual cell phone subscriptions have topped 200 million, and there is fierce competition within the wireless industry for each new customer. Service providers invest enormous amounts of money into marketing each year to ensure they convey a positive brand image, often based on customer service. Yet companies jeopardize their reputation by failing to address public concerns regarding retired cell phones.

Unlike with many other types of e-waste, cell phone recycling is profitable because many phones are refurbished and resold, while others are mined for scrap metals. The four companies reviewed by EARTHWORKS share a significant portion of the profits from their take-back programs with a variety of charities, putting a human face on their programs and adding the moral value of making a donation. When informed about responsible cell phone recycling, many consumers have expressed an interest to participate in order to benefit both the environment and a worthy cause.

Between 1999 and 2003, the leading take-back programs generated $6.4 million for such causes. However, the failure of service providers to adequately promote these programs with the public is an important missed opportunity for both company reputation and the valued charities that the programs benefit.

Steps must be taken to ensure that take-back programs avoid the serious environmental consequences of irresponsible recycling.

When consumers think about the wireless industry they first think of their service provider. These companies are at the front line of customer interaction and have an obligation to use that interface to communicate and facilitate responsible wireless recycling. Companies should capitalize on public enthusiasm by educating consumers and encouraging recycling when they are making upgrades or terminating service.

Satisfying customers and practicing good corporate citizenship involves more than just creating take-back programs.

It requires a firm company-wide commitment to promote these programs at every opportunity and to provide systems and incentives that make it easy for consumers to recycle. Steps must be taken to ensure that take-back programs avoid the serious environmental consequences of irresponsible recycling and service providers must end trade association efforts to block proactive policy solutions to this problem. Our survey, although not definitive, indicates that there is both the potential for cell phone providers to enhance their brand and image by establishing and promoting a world-class cell phone recycling program and there is also the potential for weak programs to have a negative impact.

Recommendation: Responsible Processing

All retired phones and their accessories must be processed in a manner that, at a minimum, meets the Electronics Recycler's Pledge of True Stewardship. Cell phone take-back efforts should not create more harm than good; increased collections must *not* correlate with increased dumping of toxic e-waste or an increase in the use of inefficient and polluting recovery services.

Cell phone take-back efforts should not create more harm than good; increased collections must not *correlate with increased dumping of toxic e-waste.*

ReCellular, the largest cell phone recycler in the country with approximately 53 percent of the U.S. market share, previously qualified for the Recycler's Pledge. However, in March 2005, managers of the Pledge of True Stewardship and ReCellular identified a portion of ReCellular's export sales that were inconsistent with the Pledge. Specifically, ReCellular sold used, untested cell phones to businesses in non-OECD/EU countries (members of either the European Union or the Organization for Economic Cooperation and Development). As a result, after negotiations with Pledge administrators, ReCellular eventually opted to withdraw from the Pledge.

America's leading service providers and their trade association must distance themselves from questionable practices and commit to partnering with a recycler who meets Pledge criteria, of which they have many options in the United States.

In addition to e-waste dumping, there are additional concerns related to the recycling/refurbishing process that should be addressed:

- *Thorough Testing of Phones Before Export.* Multi-step testing of phones must take place before they are exported in order to ensure that irreparable phones are not "dumped" overseas.

- *Efficiency of Waste Processing.* Recyclers must use facilities (e.g. smelters) which are located in developed countries only, and which provide the most efficient and least polluting recovery services available globally. Facilities must aim to recover the highest number of metals possible and avoid wasting valuable metals by "slagging".

- *Ability to Take-Back and Process Chargers.* A very high concentration of toxic metals exist in cell phone chargers, yet some programs do not accept them or actually penalize charities for sending them in.

- *Product Design.* Service providers should work with manufacturers to promote efficient, universal design that facilitates the recycling process, aides in portability, and extends the average 18-month lifespan of a phone.

Recommendation: Publicize and Collect More Phones

Steps must immediately be taken to dramatically increase the rate of cell phone take-back. Previous research has produced a laundry list of recommendations for improving industry take-back efforts, but these recommendations have largely been ignored.

- *The Web.* Sales, bill payment and customer service are all offered online, and customers rely on the web to find important information. Take-back programs deserve prominent placement on the company website as a service to customers, not just as a public relations campaign.

- *In Stores.* Take-back programs should be an inherent part of the services offered by a retail store—collection points should be clearly visible and promoted with signs. Representatives should have accurate information and enthusiastically share it with customers. Incentives like tax receipts and rebates have proven to increase the return of retired phones and should be widely offered.

- *On the Phone.* Representatives should be able to provide accurate information on their company's program. This information should be a basic part of every call, especially when a customer calls regarding termination of service. Information should also be featured in the announcements played while a customer waits on hold.

- *Recycling Logos.* Labeling cell phones with a universal recycling logo would help send a clear message to consumers that phones can and should be recycled.

- *Inclusion in Ad Campaigns, Billing Statements and Text Messages.* Television, radio and print media are inundated with cell phone advertisements yet do not mention take-back or recycling. Promoting programs in any of these mediums would reach millions of consumers.

- *Mail-in Options.* Pre-paid postage mail-in labels and bags help alleviate the burden on consumers, and high success has been attained with take-backs for similar products such as printer ink cartridges.

Recommendation: Better Accountability and Transparency

The wireless industry must become more accountable for their efforts by making take-back figures available to the public. Only one carrier, Verizon Wireless, posted recent data on their collection programs and amount donated to charity on their website; some had vague and outdated data, and others refused to provide information to the public. In addition, service providers should be clear and consistent when promoting their programs so that customers are not confused about how their donation is being put to use.

ReCellular, the largest and most prominent cell phone recycler, initially cited a non-disclosure agreement with their processor when asked to release information regarding their recycling practices. They subsequently disclosed where their phones are processed. The credibility of a program such as this depends on standards, public disclosure and transparency.

The industry's silence on these issues hinders government agencies and non-governmental organizations from developing an accurate picture of the problem of retired cell phones and their ability to address it.

6

Prison Recycling Programs Are Dangerous for Inmates

Kristin Jones

Kristin Jones is a fellow at the Toni Stabile Center for Investigative Journalism at Columbia University.

Prison jobs in which inmates dismantle and recycle electronic waste for pennies an hour are exposing inmates and prison employees to dangerous levels of toxic dust, which can even be spread on their clothing to contaminate others outside the prison. An investigation found that inmates were working without protective gear and that they were regularly exposed to levels of heavy metals and other toxins that were many times higher than those allowed by law. Many inmate workers believe their health problems are directly caused by the exposure, and lawsuits have been filed against the company that runs the nationwide prison recycling program. Some of the prison recycling facilities have been shut down entirely because of the problems, but others have made improvements and are still operating with better safety conditions. This article has been edited from its original form to suit this publication.

Toxic dust from an electronics recycling program run by the federal prison system may have put hundreds of inmates, workers and even their families at risk, according to preliminary findings in a two-year investigation by the Justice Department's Office of the Inspector General.

Kristin Jones, "Prison Work Program May Have Put Hundreds of Prisoners and Workers at Risk; DOJ Investigates a Prison Electronics Recycling Program," ABCnews.com, July 10, 2008. Article has been edited from its original form. Reproduced by permission.

In a letter obtained by ABC News, the Inspector General's office last November [2007] requested medical evaluations of more than 300 prisoners and workers who may have been exposed to heavy metal contamination and other hazardous materials in operations to break open computer monitors and extract components.

The ongoing investigation and findings that workers were likely exposed to toxic dust resulted in the suspension on June 27 [2008] of recycling operations at a prison in Ohio. They also may pave the way for lawsuits against the Federal Prison Industries, a government-owned corporation known as UNICOR that aims to rehabilitate prisoners through labor. One lawsuit has already been filed in Florida this spring [2008].

Some accuse the DOJ [Department of Justice] of moving too slowly and failing to remedy the potential exposure problem.

Representative Pete Hoekstra (R-Mich) said he has low expectations for the ongoing investigation. UNICOR has grown rapidly in recent decades to make nearly $858 million in net sales and employ more than 23,000 inmates last year. Hoekstra accused the Justice Department of protecting it because it is "a cash cow."

"It will result in nothing," Rep. Hoekstra told ABCNews .com. "We rail against Chinese prison labor, and what you've got here is a situation where our prisons have exposed our workers to low wages and dangerous working environments, with the full support of the Justice Department and with the full support of the White House."

Tracey Hendrix, a 39-year-old former inmate at a federal prison in Marianna, Florida, is typical of the prisoners employed by UNICOR.

Paid 33 cents an hour, more than double the 12 cents paid to the inmates who worked in the prison kitchen, she dismantled computers in a UNICOR warehouse from 1999 to 2001. UNICOR now pays inmates between 25 cents and $1.15

an hour, and employs 1200 inmates in its nationwide recycling program, according to a recent brochure.

"We didn't have nothing to put on our faces, and we just breathed and coughed all day," said Hendrix, now a resident of Birmingham, Alabama.

She did not learn about potential hazards of the dust in the warehouse until another former inmate told her that she, like Hendrix, had a miscarriage after leaving the facility. Now they believe that the exposure at UNICOR caused their health problems.

"It seemed like everyone that was working with me had a miscarriage," said Hendrix, who is considering joining a lawsuit alleging cruel and unusual punishment.

Lawsuits Are Under Way

Twenty-six inmates, UNICOR staff members, their family members and visitors to a recycling operation at Marianna have already joined a suit filed in the northern district court of Florida in March. They accuse UNICOR and the Bureau of Prisons of recklessly endangering workers and prisoners, and list medical complaints including skin lesions, lung and heart problems, cancer, short-term memory loss, miscarriages and general pain that they blame on contaminants. Local union members at a prison in Texarkana, Texas are also considering a lawsuit, according to a union representative.

"Those worries are perfectly legitimate," said Tee L. Guidotti, an occupational health expert at George Washington University's School of Public Health. The growing industry of recycling used electronics, he said, is known to be potentially hazardous.

While he could not comment on individual cases, Guidotti said that the inmates' and workers' concerns were similar to those affecting local communities in developing countries like China, where much of the world's used electronics end up. There, informal methods of breaking down computers by hand have resulted in severe health and environmental problems. Done improperly, recycling can release heavy metal dust, and certain methods of applying heat to break down electronics can amplify the effect of toxins, said Guidotti.

A spokesperson for the Bureau of Prisons, Traci Billingsley, said that the agency was committed to meeting all federal health, safety and environmental guidelines.

"Safeguards have been in place for several years at all recycling factories to ensure worker protection," said Billingsley.

Levels of airborne lead dust at the recycling facility at times reached 50 times higher than the federally accepted level for workplaces.

"These safeguards include baseline testing and medical monitoring of all staff and inmates assigned to the glass breaking operations," said Billingsley.

In interviews with ABCNews.com, many UNICOR workers agreed that conditions improved after Leroy Smith, a former safety manager at Atwater prison in Merced, California, went public in 2004 with a claim that administrators had ignored his repeated warnings. The operations to break open computer monitors now happen in ventilated glass-breaking booths, and prisoners usually wear masks, protective suits, and gloves.

'Serious Problems Remain'

But the recent Inspector General's investigation into recycling facilities at Elkton Federal Correctional Institution in Ohio showed that serious problems remain. Levels of airborne lead dust at the recycling facility at times reached 50 times higher than the federally accepted level for workplaces. During a periodic filter-change operation, the level of cadmium was 450 times higher.

Lead can cause severe damage to nervous and reproductive systems, including miscarriages, said John McKernan, an industrial hygienist at the Centers for Disease Control. Cadmium can cause lung damage and bone disease, and has been linked to cancer, he said. And other elements may also be present in used computers, including mercury and arsenic, which can cause skin lesions like those reported by many UNICOR workers.

The factories at Elkton were shuttered on June 27 [2008] for a thorough clean-up, said Billingsley, adding that this move went beyond inspectors' recommendations for gradual remediation. It is unclear when or whether the facilities will re-open, she said.

UNICOR staff "may have inadvertently exposed their families to heavy metals by wearing their dust-laden work clothes home."

Similar contamination may affect other facilities that have yet to be fully inspected, according to the November 27 [2007] letter by the office's investigative counsel S. Randall Humm to an officer at the National Institute for Occupational Safety and Health.

The risks are not limited to workers and inmates. UNICOR staff "may have inadvertently exposed their families to heavy metals by wearing their dust-laden work clothes home," wrote Humm.

That, said Guidotti, should never have happened.

"They wore their work clothes home? Yikes. That has been known for years to be a set-up for exposing children," he said.

7

Manufacturers Should Be Responsible for Their Products as E-Waste

Rick Callahan

Rick Callahan is a reporter for the Associated Press.

Because federal legislators have been slow to tackle the problem of how to handle the e-waste problem, several states have drafted their owns laws to deal with it. The majority of state e-waste laws put the burden on manufacturers for collecting and recycling their own products at the end of the product's life cycle. Companies have pushed back against such regulations, claiming that it will cost them millions of dollars annually. However, the volume of e-waste returned through collection programs in states that have implemented e-waste laws shows the need for such legislation and the success of the programs developed as a result.

Frustrated by inaction in Congress, a growing number of states are trying to reduce the rising tide of junked TVs, computers and other electronics that have become one of the nation's fastest-growing waste streams.

Nineteen states have passed laws requiring the recycling of old electronics, which contain both precious metals and toxic pollutants and are piling up in garages and closets—or worse, getting dumped overseas. Thirteen other states are considering laws.

But as these state measures take effect, the electronics industry is pushing back against what it calls a hard-to-follow "patchwork."

Two trade groups, the Consumer Electronics Association and the Information Technology Industry Council, are suing New York City over its recycling law, which will make electronics manufacturers provide free collection of electronics weighing more than 15 pounds. That includes "orphan" waste made by now-defunct manufacturers.

The groups contend the law, which requires detailed paper trails documenting their recycling, will cost their member companies more than $200 million annually.

Parker Brugge, the Consumer Electronics Association's vice president of environmental affairs and industry sustainability, said the states' laws burden manufacturers with drafting state-specific recycling plans. His group would prefer a national e-waste law that sets a uniform policy and spreads the responsibility of recycling among companies, consumers and local governments.

Barbara Kyle, national coordinator of the Electronics Takeback Coalition, a group that promotes e-waste recycling, thinks manufacturers really want a national policy with less teeth than the state laws.

Parker Brugge, the Consumer Electronics Association's vice president of environmental affairs and industry sustainability, said the states' laws burden manufacturers with drafting state-specific recycling plans.

"They talk about how much they want a federal bill, but what they want is a weak federal bill. They don't want to have to do what the state laws are making them do," she said.

Several e-waste bills have been introduced in Congress over the years but none has passed.

In April, the House authorized the Environmental Protection Agency [EPA] to award grants promoting e-waste recycling. The Senate has not yet voted on it.

Meanwhile, the amount of e-waste grows. In 2007, Americans disposed of 2.25 million tons of TVs, computers, cell phones, fax machines, printers and scanners. That's more than twice the amount generated in 1999, according to the EPA.

Less than a fifth of e-waste overall is recycled, which allows for the copper, silver, gold and other precious metals inside to be salvaged and resold. Landfills get many of the rest of the discarded devices, which also have toxic hazards lurking inside—from lead in TVs and computer monitors with cathode-ray tubes to cadmium in rechargeable batteries.

The EPA says stringent landfill regulations keep those toxic materials from posing significant threats to the nation's groundwater. But millions of tons of e-waste are shipped each year to developing nations, where scrap yards crush or burn components, exposing workers to dangerous fumes.

Most of the state e-waste laws make electronics manufacturers responsible for collecting and recycling their discarded products at little or no cost to consumers—who increasingly are being banned from setting electronics out for regular trash pickups.

Some of the laws specify how convenient companies must make it for people to dispose of old electronics, while others set collection goals companies have to meet.

Companies are generally given the flexibility to decide how they will reach those targets. They can stage periodic collection events, for instance, or they can count products collected by their own recycling programs or ones run by municipalities and nonprofits.

About half the states require electronics manufacturers to handle not only their own products but also varying amounts of the "orphan" devices that consumers drop off, said Jason Linnell, executive director of the National Center for Electronics Recycling.

Only one state, California, makes consumers pay upfront for e-waste recycling. Under its law, consumers must pay between $8 and $25 above the price of TVs, computer monitors, laptop computers and portable DVD players.

Beginning next year, companies must register with the state, pay annual fees and file reports detailing the devices they sold and how much e-waste they funneled into recycling programs.

Last year [2008], California paid $96 million collected from that fee to recyclers and collectors who handled about 218 million pounds of old electronics, said Chris Peck, spokesman for the California Integrated Waste Management Board.

In April [2009], Indiana became the latest state to pass an e-waste law. It requires makers of TVs, monitors, and laptops to recycle 60 percent of the weight of the products they sell each year in Indiana.

Beginning next year, companies must register with the state, pay annual fees and file reports detailing the devices they sold and how much e-waste they funneled into recycling programs. Companies face fines if they don't meet the 60 percent goal.

Minnesota's similar 2007 law led to about 34 million pounds of electronics—some 6.5 pounds for each state resident—being collected in its first year, said Garth Hickle, the product stewardship team leader for the Minnesota Pollution Control Agency.

One 2007 collection event at the Mall of America had to be cut short after organizers were overwhelmed by people hauling in about 1 million pounds of electronics that had been cluttering their homes.

"Some people waited in line for two hours to drop off material," Hickle said. "That just shows you that if the collection options are there, people are ready to get rid of this stuff."

Bob Davis' home and garage in Lake City, Minn., were stuffed with more than 30 old PCs and parts from his days repairing computers. Last year, Davis, 62, finally rounded them up and hauled them to a recycling business that is part of Minnesota's system.

"My wife was always yelling at me, 'When are you going to get rid of this stuff?'" Davis said. "I'd say, 'Well, when I find a place that will take it.'"

8

Consumers Should Dispose of Their E-Waste Properly

Consumer Reports

Consumer Reports, *a unit of Consumers Union, is a nonprofit organization supported by subscriptions to its magazine and website, and which publishes independent testing of products and services for use by consumers.*

States all around the country are enacting laws to regulate how electronic waste must be disposed, and many big manufacturers and retailers themselves have begun offering their own e-waste take-back and recycling programs for their customers. This means that consumers have more opportunities than ever before to do the right thing and dispose of their old electronics responsibly. When purchasing new electronics, consumers should check to see whether the retailer or manufacturer offers take-back recycling for the product; they can also find out if their town or state offers collection days for unwanted electronics. Consumers can also consider donating working electronics items to charities or other nonprofit organizations. If a private recycling firm is the only option, consumers should make sure the company is pledged to practice good stewardship.

Consumers' healthy demand for new electronic products comes with an unhealthy side effect: mountains of toxic e-waste. For example, the cathode ray tube (CRT) in every

Consumer Reports, "Think Green: Recycle Your Old Electronics—States and Companies Offer More Options for Consumers," ConsumerReports.org, April 2007.

old-style TV or computer monitor ripe for replacement contains four to eight pounds of potentially brain-damaging lead.

Even small electronic products, such as cell phones, personal stereos, and camcorders, pose big hazards. From the mercury in their batteries and the cadmium in their displays, to the arsenic in their circuit boards and the brominated flame retardants (BFR) in their housings, trashed electronics constitute a serious environmental threat when buried in landfills, leaching carcinogens and other harmful substances into groundwater.

The federal Environmental Protection Agency says it is safe to discard TVs in a properly managed landfill, although it strongly recommends recycling to promote resource conservation. In the absence of a national recycling program, many states and municipalities have banned CRTs from landfills in an effort to reduce the high costs and health risks associated with handling such materials.

With an estimated 20 to 24 million unused TVs and computers already gathering dust in homes and offices across the country, more municipal initiatives, state and local laws, and private programs run by manufacturers and retailers are trying to keep e-waste out of landfills by enabling or in some cases requiring equipment recycling.

New Recycling Laws

Among the recent legislative approaches are four laws passed in California, Maine, Maryland, and Washington.

Under a first-of-its-kind statute implemented in 2004 in Maine, manufacturers are directly billed for the cost of recycling based on the proportion of waste generated by their products. It's a step recycling proponents believe might provide an incentive for manufacturers to design longer-lasting equipment or products that are more easily recycled. Consumers pay a small fee when dropping off TV sets or computer monitors at centralized locations. The state estimates its 1.28

million residents recycle 60,000 to 100,000 TVs and computer monitors annually, according to Carole Cifrino, coordinator for product management programs in Maine's Department of Environmental Protection division of solid-waste management. As of July 2006, a provision took effect requiring municipalities to assume responsibility for providing residents with a system for delivering their unwanted TVs and CRTs to consolidation centers.

In March 2006, Washington followed Maine's example by passing recycling legislation that went even further. Its law requires manufacturers to assume the costs for collecting, transporting, and processing recycled TVs, computer systems and laptops by January 2009. Residents will not be charged for recycling old equipment, although manufacturers may pass along some of the program's expense in the form of higher prices, says Suellen Mele, program director of Washington Citizens for Resource Conservation. "But we're not anticipating any significant increase in prices," she adds.

Consumers Union, the parent company of *Consumer Reports*, supports the concept of Extended Producer Responsibility (EPR), which holds manufacturers responsible for recycling costs, requiring them to compete for the portion they pass on to consumers.

California ... instituted new waste-disposal rules in ... 2006 that make it illegal for residents to dispose of most electronic items—everything from printers, fax machines, and computer monitors to cell phones and batteries—in the trash.

Maryland took a different approach with a five-year pilot program that currently applies to computer monitors only but could be expanded to include TVs. Companies that manufacture more than 1,000 PCs per year doing business in the state must pay an initial $5,000 registration fee each year, which counties and municipalities will use to promote recycling. If the manufacturer starts a take-back program, the fee for subsequent years is reduced to $500.

In California, buyers of TVs and computer monitors pay a fee of $6 to $10 at the point of sale. The state then funnels the money into a collection and recycling system. Although the regulation promotes recycling, it creates no incentive for the electronics industry to design longer-lasting products, reuse old components, or make equipment easier to recycle, recycling proponents say.

California also instituted new waste-disposal rules in February 2006 that make it illegal for residents to dispose of most electronic items—everything from printers, fax machines, and computer monitors to cell phones and batteries—in the trash. Moreover, California is the only state so far to legislate cell phone recycling. Since July 2006, cell-phone retailers in the state have been required to take back phones from customers for recycling at no fee.

Other states are following suit. Massachusetts, Minnesota, and New Hampshire all have either implemented or passed regulations banning the disposal of CRTs from incinerators, landfills or both.

Meanwhile, in Oregon, state lawmakers will be making a second attempt to pass electronics recycling legislation. The state grappled with proposals for handling e-waste in 2005, but was unable to reach a consensus. The prospects look good for breaking the deadlock later this year [2007], however, with a law that's expected to closely mirror the legislation passed last year in neighboring Washington.

Electronics-recycling legislation is currently under consideration in 20 states and Puerto Rico, according to the Consumer Electronics Association. The issue was also addressed by several bills before the last session of Congress, including the Electronic Waste Recycling Promotion and Consumer Protection Act, which is expected to be reintroduced in 2007. The bill would provide tax credits for consumers and companies that invest in recycling infrastructures for electronics products.

Nonetheless, much work remains to be done. While there's awareness of the need to recycle CRTs and PC hardware, many other electronic products are being ignored. According to Earthworks, a Washington, D.C.-based environmental advocacy group, 98 percent of the 130 million cell phones discarded in the U.S. each year are not being recycled. This is especially unnecessary as most cellular service providers have recycling programs in place, and will accept their equipment for recycling and reuse in EPR or take-back programs.

Manufacturers' Recycling Programs

Several computer manufacturers, including Apple, Dell, and HP, also provide computer recycling and donation services. Apple offers customers purchasing new Macintosh systems free shipping and domestic recycling of their old computer systems. The company also operates a recycling collection facility at its headquarters in Cupertino, Calif., which is run as a free service for the city's residents. Apple has partnered with Metech International to let consumers and businesses recycle systems weighing up to 60 pounds for a flat fee of $30 (including shipping). Apple also provides no-fee iPod recycling services to its U.S. customers through its Apple stores. Customers returning any iPod, iPod Mini, or iPod Photo will receive a 10 percent discount toward the same-day purchase of a new iPod.

Dell began offering free computer-recycling services to buyers of new Dimension and Inspiron computer systems in 2004. The company has since become one of the industry's leading recycling proponents, and now offers free recycling of any Dell-branded product. Customers purchasing new Dell desktop or notebook PCs can recycle their obsolete PC equipment free of charge. Dell also arranges for donations of old working computer systems and components to local organizations through its partnership with the National Cristina Foundation (www.cristina.org).

If you have an obsolete but working computer, digital camera, cell phone, why not donate it to a local or national charity or other nonprofit organization?

HP also encourages consumers to donate functional computer systems through its partnership with the National Cristina Foundation, and provides customers with an online calculator to determine prices for its PC recycling service. The company's recycling fees are a bit higher than those of other manufacturers (we were quoted $46 for a PC and monitor), but customers are rewarded with e-coupons that can be used toward the purchase of HP products. HP also offers free postage-paid recycling for used HP inkjet and Laser Jet cartridges, and has partnered with the Rechargeable Battery Recycling Corporation (www.rbrc.org/call2recycle/), which provides more than 32,000 retail locations—including Best Buy, Home Depot, and Staples—for free drop-off recycling of laptop, handheld cell phone, and digital camera batteries.

Other electronics manufacturers, including Panasonic, Sharp, and Sony, sponsor recycling programs as part of the "Electronics Recycling Shared Responsibility Program," an EIA [Energy Information Administration] initiative. Member companies fund the recycling of their old products, which are gathered at one-time and ongoing collection sites.

If you have an obsolete but working computer, digital camera, cell phone, why not donate it to a local or national charity or other nonprofit organization? In many cases, you'll be able to deduct the contribution from your taxes.

A good place to start is with local schools and community centers, and charities such as Goodwill Industries and the Salvation Army. You might also try a nonprofit organization like

Recycle for Breast Cancer which accepts a wide range of working and nonworking electronic items, and even mails prepaid postage labels for most product categories. Sites such as Tech-Soup, Earth 911 and *Consumer Reports' Greener Choices* can provide you with lists of nonprofit choices. Another site, Freecycle lets you find a local neighborhood group that will help you find a new home for your unwanted electronic items.

Before you recycle or donate an old computer, be sure to reformat all hard drives or use a dedicated program designed to erase personal data. You should also delete stored numbers and personal information from any cell phones you donate or recycle, and make sure your service has been deactivated.

Voluntary recycling programs might help prevent costly legislative mandates.

What You Can Do

Whether the law mandates that manufacturers pay for recycling, or whether consumers pay a recycling fee when making a purchase, consumers ultimately foot the bill. Voluntary recycling programs might help prevent costly legislative mandates. Here are the steps we recommend you take if you decide to recycle an old TV or computer.

Check with retailers. If the equipment still works, or if you think it can be repaired, check with local thrift stores. You might not want that big old tube TV, but someone else will. If you can't find a thrift store willing to take it, find out if any local charities might be interested. Some of the sites listed in this report include links to groups that accept donated electronics. Electronics retailers are also getting into the act. Best Buy sponsors recycling events where you can drop off electronics of all kinds, from TVs to fax machines. Check their Web site to see if there is an upcoming event in your neighborhood.

Check for public programs. To see if your town sponsors collection days for TVs and other electronics, or if it has a drop-off point for electronics waste, click on the map supplied by the Electronic Industries Alliance (www.eiae.org). You can also find recyclers and recycling events in your area, and locate energy-efficient or environmentally friendlier "green" electronics, by visiting my GreenElectronics sponsored by the Consumer Electronics Association (CEA).

Consider a private recycling firm. You can also take your electronics directly to a private recycling company. But some disreputable recyclers simply ship waste overseas instead of recycling it, according to Richard Goss, director of environmental affairs for the EIA. In response to this concern, a coalition of environmental groups recently established a voluntary program known as the Electronics Recycler's Pledge of True Stewardship. Companies signing the pledge agree to prevent the export of hazardous computer components to developing countries, the disposal of waste equipment in municipal landfills and incinerators not equipped to handle it, and the use of prison labor. To locate a recycler in your area that has signed the pledge, go to the Computer TakeBack Campaign Web site.

9

The Government Must Regulate E-Waste

US Government Accountability Office

The US Government Accountability Office examines the use of public funds, evaluates federal programs and policies, and provides analyses and recommendations to Congress.

The United States does not have a comprehensive national program to recycle electronic waste. For the past decade, states have each been making their own laws regarding the regulation of e-waste, and the effect is a rather ineffective patchwork of rules and loopholes. In 2010, the US Government Accountability Office (GAO) conducted a thorough study of the issue and found that increased federal involvement would be beneficial in setting standards for e-waste collection and recycling. One of the primary questions, however, is whether federal law would set a minimum standard for e-waste protocols (which states could augment with stronger laws as they see fit), or whether it would be a fixed standard that could not be altered by the states. Not surprisingly, electronics manufacturers want a fixed standard, while the states and many environmental advocates argue for a minimum standard that can be improved upon over time.

Each year, consumers purchase millions of electronic devices, such as televisions, computers, and cell phones, and are faced with what to do with their used electronics. Recy-

US Government Accountability Office, "Electronic Waste: Considerations for Promoting Environmentally Sound Reuse and Recycling, Report to the Chairman, Committee on Science and Technology, House of Representatives," July 2010. Reproduced by permission.

cling can recover a variety of materials, including precious metals, and many electronics can be reused or contain reusable components. Yet, Environmental Protection Agency (EPA) and industry data show that tens of millions of used electronics are thrown away each year. Moreover, because used electronics often contain toxic substances, such as lead and mercury, their end-of-life management raises concerns about the potential adverse impacts on human health and the environment, particularly when used electronics are exported to countries that lack a safe recycling and disposal capacity.

The management of used electronics may be subject to a combination of federal and state regulations as well as nonregulatory, or voluntary, efforts. At the federal level, EPA regulates the handling and disposal of used electronics that qualify as hazardous waste, such as those that fail EPA's tests for toxicity. In particular, items with cathode-ray tubes (CRT), such as older televisions and computer monitors, contain significant quantities of lead. EPA also works with electronics manufacturers, retailers, and recyclers; state governments; environmental groups; and other stakeholders under partnership programs that seek to ensure the environmentally sound management of used electronics. At the state level, numerous states have enacted laws establishing electronics collection and recycling programs, including mechanisms for funding the cost of recycling. As of June 2010, 23 states had enacted some type of electronics recycling legislation. Other states have banned certain electronics from landfills or funded voluntary recycling efforts. Such efforts have increased recycling opportunities for consumers but raised concerns about the growth of a patchwork of state requirements.

In this context, GAO [Government Accountability Office] examined (1) EPA's current efforts to facilitate the environmentally sound management of used electronics; (2) the views of manufacturers, retailers, recyclers, state and local governments, and other stakeholders on the current state-by-state approach to the management of used electronics; and (3) considerations for further promoting the environmentally sound management of used electronics.

At the federal level, EPA regulates the handling and disposal of used electronics that qualify as hazardous waste.

Methodology and Limitations

To address these objectives, we reviewed EPA documents and interviewed EPA officials regarding efforts to promote the environmentally sound management of used electronics. We also interviewed representatives of an array of national organizations of stakeholders affected by or concerned with management of used electronics, including manufacturers, retailers, recyclers, state and local governments, and environmental groups. To gain insights into the impact of state electronics recycling laws, we studied in detail the programs in five states—California, Maine, Minnesota, Texas, and Washington. We selected states to represent a range of models for financing recycling programs. In addition, we selected states with recycling programs that had been in place long enough for stakeholders to provide an assessment of the impacts of the legislation. In each state, we interviewed representatives of state and local governments, collectors and recyclers of used electronics that operate under the state program as well as refurbishers of used electronics, state retail associations, and state environmental groups. During these interviews, we generally discussed the impact of state legislation on collection rates for used electronics, convenience of disposal options for consumers, and environmentally sound management of electronics collected under the state programs. We also obtained stakeholders' views on options to further promote the environmentally sound management of used electronics. While recognizing that stakeholders may benefit from state legislation, such as through an increase in business opportunities for electronics recyclers, we specifically asked about the burden (if any) created by the state-by-state approach.

We encountered a number of limitations in the availability of reliable data on the impact of the state-by-state approach on various stakeholders. For example, the five states we selected did not have data on collection and recycling rates prior to the effective dates of their laws, which would be useful to quantify the impact of their programs. Similarly, some manufacturers and other stakeholders regulated under state laws had concerns about providing us with proprietary information or did not identify compliance costs in a way that enabled us to determine the portion of costs that stems from having to comply with differing state requirements. Due to such limitations, we relied predominately on stakeholders' statements regarding how they have been impacted under the state-by-state approach. . . .

We conducted this performance audit from May 2009 to July 2010 in accordance with generally accepted government auditing standards. Those standards require that we plan and perform the audit to obtain sufficient, appropriate evidence to provide a reasonable basis for our findings and conclusions based on our audit objectives. We believe that the evidence obtained provides a reasonable basis for our findings and conclusions based on our audit objectives.

The domestic infrastructure to recycle used electronics is limited, and the major markets for both recycled commodities and reusable equipment are overseas.

Background of the Issue

The management of used electronics presents a number of environmental and health concerns. EPA estimates that only 15 to 20 percent of used electronics (by weight) are collected for reuse and recycling, and that the remainder of collected materials is primarily sent to U.S. landfills. While a survey conducted by the consumer electronics industry suggests that EPA's data may underestimate the recycling rate, the industry survey confirms that the number of used electronics thrown away each year is in the tens of millions. As a result, valuable resources contained in electronics, including copper, gold, and aluminum, are lost for future use. Additionally, while modern landfills are designed to prevent leaking of toxic substances and contamination of groundwater, research shows that some types of electronics have the potential to leach toxic substances with known adverse health effects. Used electronics may also be exported for recycling or disposal. In August 2008, we reported that, while such exports can be handled responsibly in countries with effective regulatory regimes and by companies with advanced technologies, a substantial amount ends up in countries that lack the capacity to safely recycle and dispose of used electronics.

We also have previously reported on the economic and other factors that inhibit recycling and reuse. For example, many recyclers charge fees because their costs exceed the revenue they receive from selling recycled commodities or refurbishing units. Household electronics, in particular, are typically older and more difficult to refurbish and resell, and, thus, may have less value than those from large institutions. In most states, it is easier and cheaper for consumers to dispose of household electronics at a local landfill. Moreover, as EPA and others have noted, the domestic infrastructure to recycle used electronics is limited, and the major markets for both recycled commodities and reusable equipment are overseas.

No Comprehensive National Approach

The United States does not have a comprehensive national approach for the reuse and recycling of used electronics, and previous efforts to establish a national approach have been unsuccessful. Under the National Electronics Product Stewardship Initiative, a key previous effort that was initially funded by EPA, stakeholders met between 2001 and 2004, in part to develop a financing system to facilitate reuse and recycling. Stakeholders included representatives of federal, state, and local governments; electronics manufacturers, retailers, and recyclers; and environmental organizations. Yet despite broad agreement in principle, stakeholders in the process did not reach agreement on a uniform, nationwide financing system. For example, they did not reach agreement on a uniform system that would address the unique issues related to televisions, which have longer life spans and cost more to recycle than computers. In the absence of a national approach, some states have since addressed the management of used electronics through legislation or other means, and other stakeholders are engaged in a variety of voluntary efforts.

In the 9 years that have passed since stakeholders initiated the National Electronics Product Stewardship Initiative in an ultimately unsuccessful attempt to develop a national financing system to facilitate the reuse and recycling of used electronics, 23 states have enacted some form of electronics recycling legislation. . . .

The United States does not have a comprehensive national approach for the reuse and recycling of used electronics.

As of June 2010, the remaining 27 states had not enacted legislation to establish electronics recycling programs. In some of these states, legislation concerning electronics recycling has been proposed, and some state legislatures have established commissions to study options for the management of used electronics. In addition, some of these states, as well as some of the states with recycling legislation, have banned certain used electronics, such as CRTs, from landfills. In states with no mechanism to finance the cost of recycling, some local governments that offer recycling bear the recycling costs and others charge fees to consumers. Also, some states have funded voluntary recycling efforts, such as collection events or related efforts organized by local governments. . . .

Policy Considerations

Options to further promote the environmentally sound management of used electronics involve a number of basic policy considerations and encompass many variations. For the purposes of this report, we examined two endpoints on the spectrum of variations: (1) a continued reliance on state recycling programs supplemented by EPA's partnership programs and (2) the establishment of federal standards for state electronics recycling programs. Further federal regulation of electronic waste exports is a potential component of either of these two approaches. . . .

Under a national strategy based on the establishment of federal standards for state electronics recycling programs, federal legislation would be required. For the purpose of analysis, we assumed that the legislation would establish federal standards and provide for their implementation—for example, through a cooperative federalism approach whereby states could opt to assume responsibility for the standards or leave implementation to EPA, through incentives for states to develop complying programs, or through a combination of these options. Within this alternative, there are many issues that would need to be addressed. A primary issue of concern to many stakeholders is the degree to which the federal government would (1) establish minimum standards, allowing states to adopt stricter standards (thereby providing states with flexibility but also potentially increasing the compliance burden from the standpoint of regulated entities), or (2) establish fixed standards. Further issues include whether federal standards would focus on the elements of state electronics recycling laws that are potentially less controversial and have a likelihood of achieving efficiencies—such as data collection and manufacturer reporting and registration—or would focus on all of the elements, building on lessons learned from the various states.

Minimum Standards vs. Fixed Standards

An overriding issue of concern to many stakeholders is the degree to which federal standards would be established as minimum standards, fixed standards, or some combination of the two. In this context, we have assumed that either minimum or fixed standards would, by definition, preempt less stringent state laws and lead to the establishment of programs in states that have not enacted electronics recycling legislation. Minimum standards would be intended to ensure that programs in every state met baseline requirements established by the federal government, while allowing flexibility to states that have enacted legislation meeting the minimum standards to continue with existing programs, some of which are well-established. In contrast, under fixed federal standards, states would not be able to establish standards either stricter or more lenient than the federal standards. Thus, fixed standards would offer relatively little flexibility, although states would still have regulatory authority in areas not covered by the federal standards.

As we have previously reported, minimum standards are often designed to provide a baseline in areas such as environmental protection, vehicle safety, and working conditions. For example, a national approach based on minimum standards would be consistent with the authority given to EPA to regulate hazardous waste management under the Resource Conservation and Recovery Act, which allows for state requirements that are more stringent than those imposed by EPA. Such a strategy can be an option when the national objective requires that common minimum standards be in place in every state, but stricter state standards are workable. Conversely, fixed standards are an option when stricter state standards are not workable. For example, to provide national uniformity and thereby facilitate the increased collection and recycling of certain batteries, the Mercury-Containing and Rechargeable Battery Management Act does not allow states the option of establishing more stringent regulations regarding collection, storage, and transportation, although states can adopt and enforce standards for the recycling and disposal of such batteries that are more stringent than existing federal standards under the Resource Conservation and Recovery Act.

Manufacturers Prefer Fixed Standards

Most manufacturers we interviewed told us they prefer fixed federal standards over minimum standards. For example, these manufacturers are concerned that many states would opt to exceed the minimum federal standards, leaving manufacturers responsible for complying with differing requirements, not only in the states that have electronics recycling legislation but also in the states currently without legislation. In contrast, most state government officials and environmental groups we interviewed told us that they would prefer minimum federal standards over fixed federal standards as a national approach for the management of used electronics. In addition, a representative of the National Conference of State Legislatures told us that the organization generally opposes federal preemption but accepts that in the area of environmental policy, the federal government often sets minimum standards. According to the representative, even if federal requirements were of a high standard, states may want the option to impose tougher standards if the need arises. Similarly, some legislative and executive branch officials in states with electronics recycling legislation expressed concern that federal standards for electronics recycling would be of a low standard. As a result, the officials said they want to preserve the ability of states to impose more stringent requirements.

To help address manufacturer concerns about a continuation of the state-by-state approach under minimum standards, the federal government could encourage states not to exceed those standards. For example, establishing minimum standards that are relatively stringent might reduce the incentive for states to enact or maintain stricter requirements. . . .

[Officials] want to preserve the ability of states to impose more stringent requirements.

A Strengthened Federal Role

In doing our work, we found that a potential component of either approach that we discuss for managing used electronics is a greater federal regulatory role over exports to (1) facilitate coordination with other countries to reduce the possibility of unsafe recycling or dumping and (2) address the limitations on the authority of states to regulate exports. Assuming a continuation of the factors that contribute to exports, such as a limited domestic infrastructure to recycle used electronics, an increase in collection rates resulting from electronics recycling laws, either at the state or federal level, is likely to lead to a corresponding increase in exports, absent any federal restrictions. While, as we have previously noted, exports can be handled responsibly in countries with effective regulatory regimes and by companies with advanced technologies, some of the increase in exports may end up in countries that lack safe recycling and disposal capacity. . . .

According to EPA officials, a greater federal regulatory role over exports resulting from ratification of the Basel Convention would require an increase in EPA's programmatic and enforcement resources, such as additional staff. The additional resources would be needed to enable the Administrator to determine whether proposed exports will be conducted in an environmentally sound manner and to implement the Basel

Convention's notice-and-consent requirement. Moreover, the European Union's experience under the waste electrical and electronic equipment directive, which contains an obligation for waste equipment to be treated in ways that avoid environmental harm, demonstrates the need to couple the regulation of exports with enforcement efforts. A European Commission report estimated that 50 percent of waste equipment that is collected is probably not being treated in line with the directive's objectives and requirements, and that a large volume of waste may be illegally shipped to developing countries, where it is dumped or recycled in ways that are dangerous to human health and the environment.

Conclusions

Broad agreement exists among key stakeholders that reusing and recycling electronics in an environmentally sound manner has substantial advantages over disposing of them in landfills or exporting them to developing countries in a manner that threatens human health and the environment. There has been much debate over the best way to promote environmentally sound reuse and recycling, however, and any national approach may entail particular advantages and disadvantages for stakeholders. While empirical information about the experiences of states and other stakeholders in their efforts to manage used electronics can inform this debate, the question of a national approach revolves around policy issues, such as how to balance the need to ensure that recycling occurs nationwide as well as industry's interests in a uniform, national approach with states' prerogatives to tailor used electronics management toward their individual needs and preferences. In the end, these larger policy issues are matters for negotiation among the concerned parties and for decision making by Congress and the administration.

At the same time, there are a number of beneficial actions that the federal government is already taking that, as currently devised, do not require the effort and implications of new legislation, but rather would complement any of the broader strategies that policymakers might ultimately endorse. In particular, EPA's collaborative efforts—including Plug-In To eCycling, the R2 practices, EPEAT [Electronic Product Environmental Assessment Tool], and the Federal Electronics Challenge—have demonstrated considerable potential and, in some cases, quantifiable benefits. However, these programs' achievements have been limited or uncertain, and EPA has not systematically analyzed the programs to determine whether their impact could be augmented. Moreover, EPA has not developed an integrated strategy that articulates how the programs, taken together, can best assist stakeholders to achieve the environmentally responsible management of used electronics.

A key issue of national significance to the management of used electronics is how to address exports—an issue that, according to many stakeholders, would most appropriately be addressed at the federal level. EPA has taken useful steps by developing a legislative package for ratification of the Basel Convention, as we recommended in 2008. However, EPA has not yet worked with other agencies, including the State Department and the Council on Environmental Quality, to finalize a proposal for the administration to provide to Congress for review and consideration. While there are unresolved issues regarding the environmentally sound management of used electronics under the Basel Convention, providing Congress with a legislative package for ratification could provide a basis for further deliberation and, perhaps, resolution of such issues.

We recommend that the Administrator of EPA undertake an examination of the agency's partnership programs for the management of used electronics. The analysis should examine how the impacts of such programs can be augmented, and should culminate in an integrated strategy that articulates how the programs, taken together, can best assist stakeholders in achieving the environmentally responsible management of used electronics nationwide.

In addition, we recommend that the Administrator of EPA work with other federal agencies, including the State Department and the Council on Environmental Quality, to finalize a legislative proposal that would be needed for ratification of the Basel Convention, with the aim of submitting a package for congressional consideration.

10

The E-Waste Problem Is Greatly Exaggerated

Angela Logomasini

Angela Logomasini is the director of Risk and Environmental Policy at the Competitive Enterprise Center, a nonprofit public policy organization dedicated to advancing the principles of free enterprise and limited government.

Much of the e-waste legislation being considered or enacted today in the United States and Europe is based on assumptions and media hype. Laws to force electronics recycling or to regulate the chemicals in computer parts may actually do more harm than good for the environment and for consumers. For example, banning so-called toxic flame-retardants in computer casings may have the effect of increasing the fire risk for home computers and laptops; substituting weaker tin solder for toxic-but-reliable lead solder could mean parts wear out faster and units have to be replaced more often; and forcing take-back recycling could mean that more wastes find their way into the environment as companies try to comply with the rules. Governments should leave this issue alone and let the private sector handle it. Leading electronics manufacturers are doing a great job of setting the standard for recycling through voluntary, fee-based, or free programs. If allowed to run its course, the free market will see that the best solution to e-waste becomes the norm.

Increasingly, news reports and environmental activists are claiming that we are facing a new solid waste crisis. "Electronic junk [is] piling up everywhere, creating what some ex-

Angela Logomasini, "Electronic Waste," CEI.org, 2008. Reproduced by permission.

perts predict will be the largest toxic waste problem of the 21st century," reads an article in *Environmental Health Perspectives*. Similarly, Greenpeace claims, "The world is consuming more and more electronic products every year. This has caused a dangerous explosion in electronic scrap (e-waste) containing toxic chemicals and heavy metals that cannot be disposed of or recycled safely." As a result of such rhetoric, Europe has passed several "e-waste" laws, U.S. states have begun looking into their own regulations, and members of Congress have proposed legislation. Unfortunately, misinformation about the issue and the naive belief that government is positioned to improve electronic waste handling is leading to misguided policies and legislation.

In 2003, the European Union (EU) passed a couple of e-waste policies that are becoming models for U.S. regulation. The Directive on the Restriction of the Use of Certain Hazardous Substances (RoHS) phases out certain "hazardous substances"—lead, mercury, cadmium, hexavalent chromium, bromated flame retardants—that are used in electronics. The other directive, the Waste Electronic and Electrical Equipment [WEEE] Directive, mandates that companies take back electronic equipment for disposal starting in 2005.

Costs vs. Benefits

The costs of these programs are likely to be significant. The EU government estimates that both programs will cost €500 million to €900 million, and industry estimates costs of up to €62.5 billion. According to Gartner Inc., a U.K.-based technology analysis company, the cost of the two directives will raise personal computer prices by about $60.

The benefits of the programs are assumed, rather than assessed through any comprehensive study. Instead, these programs are based on the precautionary principle, which assumes that in the absence of information about risk, regulators should act to prevent potential risks.

Following Europe's lead, several members of Congress formed an e-waste task force in 2005 to study the issue and produce legislation. Members of this task force are basing their policy on misinformation, as is apparent from their comments on the topic in the press.

During the 109th Congress, several members offered e-waste legislation. Representative Juanita Millender-McDonald (D-CA) introduced H.R. 4316 and Senator Ron Wyden (D-OR) introduced S. 510, both of which would provide tax credits for recycling computers and would ban disposal of computer monitors in landfills, among other things. Representative Mike Thompson (D-CA) offered H.R. 425, which would impose a tax on electronic equipment sales, levying up to $10 per item. The funds would go to the U.S. Environmental Protection Agency (EPA), which would use them to award grants to parties working to recycle computers.

The recycling mandates ... may actually mean more air, water and solid waste pollution as products are collected, sorted and recycled.

In addition, numerous states are following Europe's lead. For example, in 2001, California banned the disposal of computer monitors in landfills, and in 2003, it passed a law to place a sales tax on computers—which lawmakers euphemistically call an "advance disposal fee." This new tax is supposed to fund a state computer recycling program, but if costs of the program grow, the state can increase the tax to cover its costs. The fee is likely to grow, because it costs about $20 to $25 to recycle each unit. Some program supporters advocate increasing the tax to as much as $60 per computer sold. E-waste policies are also in place in Maine, Maryland, Minnesota, Washington State, Connecticut, Oregon, North Carolina, and Texas.

Fundamental Problems with the Policies

Despite claims to the contrary, there are many problems with the EU e-waste programs and the U.S. versions of these laws. The recycling mandates, like those under Europe's WEEE program, may actually mean more air, water, and solid waste pollution as products are collected, sorted, and recycled. In fact, the U.K. Department of Trade and Industry notes, "For certain items, [the directive] may not be the best practicable environmental option."

In addition, WEEE presents some serious practical problems associated with collecting and recycling all the products concerned. When the EU implemented a similar program for refrigerators in 1998, the products were collected but there was nowhere to recycle them, leading to a massive stockpiling of refrigerators, now known as the "fridge fiasco." An estimated 6,500 refrigerators piled up daily—2.4 million annually. According to the U.K. government, the cost of managing these wastes was €75 million. WEEE's impacts could be much worse. According to the U.K. Environment Agency, "Fridges are just one tiny part of the WEEE directive—if we think we have problems now, then we ain't seen nothing yet." Retailers are already having a problem complying with WEEE's take back and recycling mandates. California had similar problems associated with stockpiling when it banned the disposal in landfills of computer monitors.

Likewise, RoHS-styled bans on substances used in electronic products are problematic for a number of reasons. First, they ignore important benefits of the so-called hazardous substances that are being banned—benefits that may make final products safer and longer lasting. Moreover, the risks of these substances can be managed without banning them completely.

Ironically, the risks created by the RoHS program itself may be more problematic than the risks it attempts to control. Consider the ban on using lead as solder in computers.

Lead is banned for this purpose even though there are no proven problems associated with using lead in computers. However, the substance conveys many benefits, which substitute substances might not deliver.

For one thing, lead solder is very energy efficient; it requires less energy than alternatives because it melts at low temperatures. According to a U.K. Trade and Industry study, substitutes increase energy usage by 6 to 18 percent. Similarly, a University of Stuttgart study of substitutes for lead solder indicates that the environmental impacts of the substitutes—carbon emissions, acidification, human toxicity, and ozone depletion—are all significantly higher than those for lead.

Considering Substitutes

Moreover, substitutes are likely to reduce product performance and reliability. For example, tin solder forms tiny strains called whiskers when too much moisture is present; these whiskers can spread along circuit boards and produce short-out failures. Other substitute solders are not strong enough; they consistently fail stress tests and shorten computer life, thereby increasing e-waste. Such problems are currently being cited as firms attempt to comply with RoHS. For example, one firm notes:

"Worse still, standards bodies have already discovered some serious technical misgivings about the long-term performance of lead-free, high tin alternatives such as SAC alloys. What is known so far is that lead-free solders are certainly not a 'drop in' solution for their lead forefathers. This presents a daunting prospect for many manufacturers, particularly those making high-reliability products used in safety critical applications where failure puts lives at risk. . . . Independent studies—involving exhaustive test programs to evaluate the performance of lead-free alloys in high reliability systems—have revealed situations where lead-free alloys directly compromise electronic circuit reliability."

Similar problems are associated with the ban on bromated flame retardants. These were banned because they allegedly release dangerous levels of dioxin. Yet the EU risk assessment on the topic found "no identifiable risk." There were similar findings in studies conducted by the National Academy of Sciences, the World Health Organization, and the U.S. Consumer Product Safety Commission. Yet the absence of such flame retardants presents an increased risk of fires. A Swedish study found that existing limits on the flame retardants in Europe may explain a higher number of television fires in Europe: There are currently about 165 fires per million televisions in Europe. Meanwhile, in the United States, where flame retardants are used in televisions, there are only five fires per million television sets.

In contrast to the many problems with government recycling programs, private efforts to recycle computers have proven much more effective.

Ongoing Private Computer Recycling

In contrast to the many problems with government recycling programs, private efforts to recycle computers have proven much more effective. In 2004, Dell, Hewlett-Packard, and IBM collected and recycled 160 million pounds of computer equipment. These programs are voluntary, fee-based, and affordable. At this point, Dell recycles computers for $10. (This service provides users with an airway bill for shipping the computer to Dell.)

Ironically, Representative Thompson's bill would tax consumers who buy computers to provide grants to fund computer recycling—but computer recycling is already occurring in the private sector. The difference is that the private initiatives operate without taxing consumers and charge only those who dispose of waste, not everyone who buys a computer. If the Thompson bill passed into law, it could have undermined the productive private efforts by replacing them with a less efficient government program.

Despite claims to the contrary, there is no real e-waste crisis, and the risks and costs of e-waste are manageable. Government programs promise to promote inefficiencies, increase environmental problems, and hinder market solutions. Market forces can and will produce optimal management of e-waste—if only the regulators allow them.

11

Electronics Recycling Standards Often Fall Short

Robert Houghton

Robert Houghton is president of Redemtech, a company that helps organizations responsibly manage their technology assets and electronic waste.

With all of the recent media exposure about the illegal and dangerous exporting and dumping of electronic waste, manufacturers are scrambling to make themselves look like responsible environmental stewards. Industry heavyweights, working with the US Environmental Protection Agency, have established a recycling certification known as R2 for "Responsible Recycling." Trouble is, it does not mean very much for a product to carry the R2 label. The R2 standard falls far short of the rigorous e-Stewards certification, and it lacks the support of the environmental community as well as many in the recycling industry itself. R2 is little more than an attempt at greenwashing—that is, industry players have created a certification with low, meaningless standards to give themselves the appearance of ecological legitimacy. The electronics recycling industry can do much better, and it is in its own best interest to hold itself to the highest standard for environmental stewardship. Only in this way will the use of personal electronics and other high tech products be sustainable over the long term.

We are still sending toxic e-waste to developing countries, a poisonous trade that is legal and prolific. But now that *60 Minutes, Frontline, National Geographic, 20/20* and others have mainstreamed pictures of children playing amid piles of smoldering electronic scrap, the marketplace has firmly proclaimed what the electronics industry has never been willing to say—enough!

After decades of looking the other way, the electronics manufacturers and scrap metal recyclers association (ISRI), facilitated by the EPA [Environmental Protection Agency], are rushing to make a virtue of necessity by promoting a new electronics recycling certification. Called "R2," for "Responsible Recycling," it has been tailored to serve the electronics industry's special interests.

Meanwhile, a competing certification—"e-Stewards"—has been developed by a group of concerned electronics recyclers under the auspices of the Basel Action Network, an environmental organization with the singular mission of eliminating the toxic trade in e-waste with developing countries. Many of us involved in the development of the e-Stewards standard have been long-term evangelists for truly responsible recycling, which to us means: "No export of hazardous e-waste to developing countries, domestic recycling instead of disposal in incinerators or landfills, and no use of prison labor."

Irresistible market and political pressures are forcing the electronics manufacturers and ISRI to come green, and they are desperate to make R2 a monopoly standard to ensure that they control the definition of what constitutes "responsible recycling." R2 is their blueprint for how that definition should serve their interests:

- R2 allows the export of untested electronics anywhere in the world so long as they are designated for resale and/or recycling in conformity with "R2 practices." In the absence of effective enforcement, R2 is virtually an open door to e-waste dumping.

- R2's list of controlled "focus materials" omits many toxic substances injurious to human health and the environment.

- R2 ignores the common practice of using prison labor for manual dismantling, whether in the United States or abroad—an invitation for sweatshop recycling.

- R2 does not require an independently audited Environmental Management System consistent with ISO 14001 [environmental management standards], and lacks detailed guidance documentation for implementation. So the standard will be whatever the local R2 auditor says it is. The thoroughness gap is obvious by merely comparing the lengths of the two standards: R2—15 pages; e-Stewards—49 pages, not including ISO proprietary content and a 67-page guidance document.

R2 lacks the support of the environmental community and some of the most prominent electronics recyclers in the United States.

- R2 allows incineration for "energy recovery," when recycling is not "economically feasible," ensuring much of the plastic not burned in open fields abroad will go up smokestacks here at home. "Land disposal" is similarly permitted—another common destination for hard-to-recycle plastics that make up over 60 percent of many electronics by weight.

- R2 does not require that all of a recycler's locations be certified, allowing recyclers to represent themselves as "R2 Certified" but behave however they wish in their unaudited facilities.

A Conflict of Interest

It's hard to argue with the moneyed interests behind R2, but their tactics suggest that its proponents do not consider themselves to be on the moral high ground: I have personally spoken with recyclers who report being threatened by the manufacturers they serve with a complete loss of business if they adopt the e-Stewards standard. Manufacturers are unwilling to close the door on hazardous exports to developing countries if responsible domestic recycling costs more.

The President of ISRI recently drafted a letter to the Chairman of the Congressional House Administration Committee in which he misrepresented the e-Stewards standard as having been "developed in a vacuum." In fact, the standard was developed with the input of leading recyclers and environmentalists in the industry, only after it was clear that the R2 standard would be deficient.

R2 lacks the support of the environmental community and some of the most prominent electronics recyclers in the United States. In fact, a number of recyclers now pursuing e-Stewards Certification were once participants in the R2 development process and walked away when it became clear that the manufacturers' special interests would prevail over truly responsible recycling practices.

Like R2, the e-Stewards standard has been accredited by ANSI-ASQ National Accreditation Board (ANAB) as a third-party auditable standard. I am pleased to report that Redemtech has completed its stage-2 e-Stewards certification audit, and that all nine of our facilities worldwide will be certified as e-Stewards ISO 14001 in the near future.

It is truly regrettable that only media exposure of the toxic e-waste trade finally motivated the electronics recycling industry to move toward greater responsibility.

Consumers Demand Sustainability

Certification is good in general for enterprise customers because it reduces the cost and increases the effectiveness of vendor governance and audit. It will ensure greater transparency from the electronics recycling industry. Companies concerned with issues of social and environmental responsibility should review the competing standards to judge which one unambiguously aligns with its policies. Every business is feeling the demand from its customers to be more sustainable, so it is in everyone's interests to hold the electronics industry to account for its environmental performance.

It is truly regrettable that only media exposure of the toxic e-waste trade finally motivated the electronics recycling industry to move toward greater responsibility. This is no time to tolerate special interest loopholes and grey areas.

12

E-Waste Recycling Certification Will Help Stem the Illegal Waste Trade

Environment News Service

Environment News Service is a news agency that reports on environmental issues around the world.

One of the biggest problems involved with electronic waste is that even when consumers or businesses try to do the right thing and properly recycle their old electronics, the goods often do not ultimately make it to a reputable dismantling center. Although they may put on a good front, many e-waste recyclers are little more than fly-by-night operators who simply collect the electronics and then cheaply ship them off to developing countries, where they are dumped and unsafely taken apart. To stop this practice, the business community and environmental leaders established the e-Stewards Certification and Standard, a designation that means a company is upholding the highest standard of environmental stewardship and social responsibility in its e-waste management practices. When consumers or businesses need to get rid of old electronics, they should make sure that they give their e-waste only to recycling firms that have the e-Stewards Certification and that have pledged to follow its rigorous standards.

The Natural Resources Defense Council [NRDC] Tuesday [February 9, 2010] announced its endorsement of the first certification program for electronics recycling. The new

Environment News Service, "Certification for Electronic Waste Recycling Gathers Support," ens-newswire.com, February 10, 2010. Reproduced by permission.

e-Stewards Certification relies on independent, third-party auditors to verify safe and ethical disposal of the hundreds of tons of unwanted electronics discarded every year in North America.

Created jointly by the environmental community and business leaders, the new e-Stewards Certification and Standard is held by the nonprofit Basel Action Network.

"NRDC recognised that we have finally created a principled yet practical solution to e-waste recycling that environmentalists, businesses and consumers can all embrace," said Jim Puckett, executive director of the Basel Action Network. "We are thrilled to receive NRDC's coveted endorsement in the lead-up to our global launch."

The first companies to receive e-Steward Enterprise designations as well as the first Certified e-Steward recyclers will be announced in March [2010].

The e-Stewards Standard is seen as an effective way to control the flood of hazardous old computers, TVs, monitors and other electronic waste shipped to developing countries for dismantling.

These e-Stewards are North American electronics recyclers and asset managers who have been qualified as upholding the highest standard of environmental and social responsibility.

By March 1, accredited certifying bodies will independently assure conformity to the e-Stewards Standard. The criteria include no toxic e-waste dumped in landfills or incinerators, exported to developing countries, or sent to prison labor operations and accountability for the entire recycling chain of toxic materials.

The e-Stewards Standard is seen as an effective way to control the flood of hazardous old computers, TVs, monitors and other electronic waste shipped to developing countries for dismantling.

"This initiative is sorely needed," said NRDC senior scientist Dr. Allen Hershkowitz. "Many e-waste recyclers claim to be green, but in reality they rely on unsafe and ecological damaging methods like dumping millions of tons of toxic waste each year in China, India and Africa. E-Stewards provide businesses and consumers with a first-of-a-kind seal to identify the truly responsible recyclers."

Electronic equipment contains toxics such as mercury, lead, cadmium, arsenic, beryllium, and brominated flame retardants. When burned, even more dangerous toxics can be formed such as dioxins and polycyclic aromatic hydrocarbons that can cause cancer and birth defects.

While there is some gold and platinum in obsolete electronics, there is not enough to cover the costs of responsibly managing it in developed countries. For this reason, it is exported to countries where workers are paid low wages and the infrastructure and legal framework is too weak to protect the environment, workers and communities.

The truly responsible recyclers in the U.S. and Canada face unfair competition from the thousands of unethical, so-called 'waste recyclers' in North America that would more accurately be called waste shippers.

The Basel Action Network explains that sending equipment and parts for reuse is "an important solution" that can be abused by falsely labeling scrap as reusable or repairable equipment. Often this scrap equipment ends up getting dumped in countries lacking any infrastructure to properly manage it.

A Call for Compliance

The NRDC and Basel Action Network are calling on all electronics recyclers to become e-Steward Certified recyclers.

They are asking all businesses to become designated "e-Steward Enterprises" by agreeing to give priority to e-Steward recyclers for their old electronic assets.

The e-Stewards Certification and Standard program will feature an ANSI-ASQ National Accreditation Board certification system with third-party auditing. The funding to create the certification program was provided by the 14 recycling companies designated as e-Steward Founders.

The e-Steward Founders are Boliden AB, California Electronic Asset Recovery, Cascade Asset Management, ECS Refining, Electronic Recyclers International, GreenCitizen, Hesstech, Metech, Redemtech, RELectronics, the Surplus Exchange, Total Reclaim, Waste Management Recycle America, and WeRecycle!.

"Currently, the truly responsible recyclers in the U.S. and Canada face unfair competition from the thousands of unethical, so-called 'waste recyclers' in North America that would more accurately be called waste shippers," said Neil Peters-Michaud of e-Steward Founder, Cascade Asset Management.

"We strongly support a certified, audited program to separate the legitimate recyclers from the low-road operators," he said. "We urge consumers and businesses to only use qualified e-Stewards and thus make sure that their old electronics are being safely recycled here at home."

Already there are about 50 recyclers that are considered "Pledged e-Stewards." Some of the largest electronics recyclers in North America, these companies have been vetted by Basel Action Network and are licensed and committed to becoming certified within the next 18 months.

13

Precious Metals from E-Waste Could Be Tomorrow's Jewelry

Dean Irvine

Hong-Kong-based writer Dean Irvine is a digital producer for CNN.com.

Gold medals at the 2010 Winter Olympic Games were solid proof of the value of the motto "reduce, reuse, recycle"—they contained gold that was reclaimed from electronic waste such as computers. Even though it was just a small amount, the journey from e-waste to Olympic medal shows that precious metals such as gold cannot only be responsibly recovered but also successfully repurposed from today's cast-away electronics. As they say, one person's junk is another's treasure, and—with new technologies and a good profit motive—extracting precious metals from e-waste could create a new global industry of green economy jobs. Today's broken laptop could well find a second life as tomorrow's earrings or other gold-containing product.

The champions at the Winter Olympic Games in Vancouver can stand on the podium proud of their achievements, but the eco-minded among them can be extra proud that their medals are made with traces of precious metals recovered from e-waste.

The amounts may be tiny (just 1.52 percent in the gold medals) but they provide a shiny example of how precious metals recovered from disused circuit boards from electronic devices can be re-used.

Dean Irvine, "Can E-Waste Be Turned to Gold?" CNN.com, February 24, 2010. Courtesy CNN. Reproduced by permission.

According to a new report, however, a more universal solution to a growing problem needs to be found.

The report published this week [February 24, 2010] by the United Nations Environment Programme (UNEP) says that in 10 years e-waste from old computers is set to increase by 400 percent in China and South Africa from 2007 levels, and by 500 percent in India.

Based on 11 countries in Asia, Africa and Latin America the report warns that in countries with relatively little e-waste today—such as Kenya, Peru, Senegal and Uganda—it will soon be a huge problem. Those nations can expect e-waste to increase from PCs alone four-fold by 2020.

Around 40 million tons of e-waste are produced each year, with much of it unaccounted for, according to findings by Solving The E-waste Problem (Steps), a UN-initiative supported by many major electronics companies.

While often dumping grounds for e-waste exported from the EU [European Union] and the U.S., countries such as China and India also will have to deal with a huge growth in home-produced e-waste fueled by a boom in sales of electronics.

The UNEP report states that much of the e-waste in developing economies is not handled safely, often incinerated and exposing workers and the local environment to hazardous chemicals and toxins.

"China is not alone in facing a serious challenge. India, Brazil, Mexico and others may also face rising environmental damage and health problems if e-waste recycling is left to the vagaries of the informal sector," Achim Steiner, Executive Director of UNEP said in the report.

According to Steps, China has 2 million of these backyard dismantlers and recyclers, far greater than the official regulated sector.

Solutions for Both Short and Long Term

"We need to find a way to keep them in the business to earn a living. E-waste recycling is a rather complex process requiring a lot of capacity, technologies and knowledge," said Ruediger Kuehr, of the United Nations University. "But easy steps can be taken so people and the environment in the informal sector don't suffer harm."

Kuehr believes most of the short-term solutions come from better training and infrastructure for the informal sector workers, but longer term needs more international coordination and better local enforcement.

One person's waste can be another's raw material.

If done correctly it could be a money-spinner for those involved in every part of e-waste disposal and recycling operations.

"One person's waste can be another's raw material. The challenge of dealing with e-waste represents an important step in the transition to a green economy," Konrad Osterwalder, U.N. under-secretary general, said in the report.

"Smart new technologies and mechanisms, which, combined with national and international policies, can transform waste into assets, creating new businesses with decent green jobs. In the process, countries can help cut pollution linked with mining and manufacturing, and with the disposal of old devices."

One idea is to put greater responsibility on the companies that produce the goods, which Kuehr suggests could be in their long-term interests as well.

"Instead of purchasing the product, we are only purchasing the service the product provides. So it's then in the interests of the companies to see the equipment returned from the consumer when they have new developments. It's a different system. It shifts responsibility from the consumer to the producer."

How much money are we wasting here by not properly recycling and letting it go to landfills?

In the short term, it may be that Winter Olympic champions remain in the minority of those safely getting their hands on e-waste gold. Yet the amount of money involved and greater awareness makes Kuehr hopeful they won't be the only ones.

"How much money are we wasting here by not properly recycling and letting it go to landfills? If we only look at the PC sector, it is gold worth in the hundreds of millions that we are wasting," he said.

Organizations to Contact

The editors have compiled the following list of organizations concerned with the issues debated in this book. The descriptions are derived from materials provided by the organizations. All have publications or information available for interested readers. The list was compiled on the date of publication of the present volume; the information provided here may change. Be aware that many organizations take several weeks or longer to respond to inquiries, so allow as much time as possible.

Basel Action Network (BAN)
206 First Ave. S., Suite 410, Seattle, WA   98104
(206) 652-5555 • fax: (206) 652-5750
website: www.ban.org

The Basel Action Network is focused on confronting the global environmental injustice and economic inefficiency of toxic trade (toxic wastes, products, and technologies) and its devastating impacts. The group actively promotes sustainable and just solutions to the consumption and e-waste crises, banning waste trade while promoting green, toxic-free, and democratic design of consumer products. BAN's website gathers up-to-date e-waste news articles from a variety of international sources, and also offers a photo gallery, reports, speeches, and even poetry on the subject.

Competitive Enterprise Institute
1899 L St. NW, Floor 12, Washington, DC   20036
(202) 331-1010 • fax: (202) 331-0640
e-mail: info@cei.org
website: www.cei.org

The Competitive Enterprise Institute, founded in 1984, is a nonprofit public policy organization dedicated to advancing the principles of free enterprise and limited government. CEI argues that the best solutions to environmental problems come from individuals making their own choices in a free marketplace. It publishes opinion and analysis pieces on its online *Daily Update* and the electronic newsletter *CEI Planet*.

Dell Earth

(800) 915-3355

e-mail: environment_policy@dell.com

website: http://content.dell.com/us/en/corp/dell-earth.aspx

Founded in 1984, Dell is a technology-based company that manufactures and sells computers and other equipment around the world. On its Dell Earth web page, the company describes its recovery and recycling programs, energy efficient products, and safe and environmentally preferred materials. The site also offers "Direct2Dell," a blog that discusses environmental topics, an environmental RSS feed, videos, and wallpaper. In 2010, *Newsweek* magazine named Dell the "greenest," or most environmentally responsible, company in America.

Earthworks/Recycle My Cell Phone

1612 K St. NW, Suite 808, Washington, DC   20006

(202) 887-1872

e-mail: info@earthworksaction.org

website: www.recyclemycellphone.org/resources.shtml

Earthworks is a nonprofit organization dedicated to protecting communities and the environment from the destructive impacts of mineral development worldwide. Through its grassroots "Recycle My Cell Phone" campaign, the organization partners with a responsible recycler to accept and either refurbish or recycle old cell phones, PDAs, and pagers using the highest environmental and social standards. The RecycleMy CellPhone.org website has full details on how to send in a phone for recycling, as well as useful factsheets about cell phone e-waste.

Ecology Action

877 Cedar St., Suite 240, Santa Cruz, CA   95060
(831) 426-5925 • fax: (831) 425-1404
website: www.ecoact.org

Established in 1970, Ecology Action is a nonprofit environmental consultancy delivering education services, technical assistance, and program implementation for initiatives that assist individuals, businesses, and governments in the Santa Cruz, California, area to maximize environmental quality and community wellbeing. Although many of its programs are locally based, Ecology Action's "E-Waste Electronic Recycling Program" web page offers educational information, press releases, and links to national electronics manufacturers' recycling programs.

Electronics TakeBack Coalition (ETBC)

60 29th St., Suite 230, San Francisco, CA   94110
(415) 206-9595
e-mail: info@etakeback.org
website: www.electronicstakeback.com/home/

A project of the nonprofit Tides Center, the Electronics Take-Back Coalition promotes green design and responsible recycling in the electronics industry. Its goal is to protect the health and wellbeing of electronics users, workers, and the communities where electronics are produced and discarded by requiring electronics manufacturers and brand owners to take full responsibility for the life cycle of their products, through effective public policy requirements or enforceable agreements. The ETBC website prominently features "The Story of Electronics," an animated film by Annie Leonard that is the sequel to 2007's popular "Story of Stuff" webfilm, viewed eight million times by people in 223 countries. The site also offers a variety of informative reports and news items about e-waste, as well as its *2010 Recycling Scorecard* and a consumer guide for buying greener electronics.

Greenpeace

702 H St. NW, Suite 300, Washington, DC   20001
(202) 462-1177
e-mail: info@wdc.greenpeace.org
website: www.greenpeace.org/usa/

Founded in 1971, Greenpeace is an international organization that uses peaceful direct action and creative communication to address global environmental problems. Greenpeace International releases an annual *Guide to Greener Electronics*, which was expanded in 2007 to include televisions and computer games. The guide ranks consumer electronics companies based on the removal of toxic chemicals from their products and company recycling initiatives. The latest edition exposes the widening gap between companies that make good on their promises to clean up, and those that do not.

Hewlett-Packard Company (HP)

3000 Hanover St., Palo Alto, CA   94304-1185
(650) 857-1501 • fax: (650) 857-5518
website: http://welcome.hp.com/country/us/en/cs/home
_c.html

Hewlett-Packard Company, founded in 1939, is the world's largest manufacturer and seller of computer hardware. On its "HP and the Environment" web page, it offers tips for using and disposing of electronics responsibly, a collection of news articles and press releases, and a "Designing for the Environment" video. A "Recycling and Reuse" page provides information about how and where to recycle, refurbish, or donate the company's products.

Institute of Scrap Recycling Industries (ISRI)

1615 L St. NW, Suite 600, Washington, DC   20036-5610
(202) 662-8500 • fax: (202) 626-0900
website: www.isri.org

The Institute of Scrap Recycling Industries is the voice of the scrap recycling industry, an association of more than 1,350 companies that process, broker, and consume scrap commodities. Based in Washington, DC, the group encourages manufacturers to build electronics with safer, more easily recyclable materials, and educates the public about the benefits of scrap recycling. ISRI publishes a bimonthly magazine, *Scrap*, and maintains a collection of reports, letters, and position papers on its website, which includes a section dedicated to electronics recycling issues.

Silicon Valley Toxics Coalition (SVTC)

760 North First St., Suite 200, San Jose, CA   95112
(408) 287-6707 • fax: (408) 287-6771
e-mail: svtc@svtc.org
website: www.svtc.org

Silicon Valley Toxics Coalition is a nonprofit organization engaged in research, advocacy, and grassroots organizing to promote human health and environmental justice in response to the rapid growth of the high-tech industry. In partnership with national and international non-governmental organizations, SVTC works to keep electronics from being exported or sent to prisons for "recycling" and advocates for the reduction and eventual elimination of noxious chemicals in electronic products. SVTC publishes a quarterly newsletter, and its website offers a wide variety of reports, fact sheets, legal updates, and videos about e-waste and other environmental issues related to high technology.

Swiss Federal Institute of Technology

ETH Zurich HG, Rämistrasse 101, Zürich   8092
   Switzerland
+41 44 632 11 11 • fax: +41 44 632 10 10
website: http://ewasteguide.info/

Through a program called Empa, the Swiss Federal Institute of Technology is a pioneer in monitoring and control for e-waste management systems. Empa leads several projects in Asia, Africa, and Latin America, helping to build capacities for e-waste management in areas of policy and legislation, business and financing, and technology and skills. It has been instrumental in helping to develop a global knowledge sharing platform on e-waste. It maintains an extensive "e-waste guide" on its website, offering statistics, reports, a bibliography, and a link to subscribe to an e-mail newsletter, "Ewasteguide.info."

US Environmental Protection Agency (EPA)
Office of Resource Conservation and Recovery (5305P)
1200 Pennsylvania Ave. NW, Washington, DC   20460
website: www.epa.gov

Established in 1970, the US Environmental Protection Agency leads the nation's environmental science, research, education, and assessment efforts. The EPA maintains a web page dedicated to "ecycling" on its website, offering basic information about reducing electronics waste, frequent questions and answers about e-waste, publications that offer information about e-waste, related links that include resources for recycling and donation programs, and information about market trends in e-waste generation and recovery.

Zero Waste America (ZWA)
217 South Jessup St., Philadelphia, PA   19107
(215) 629-3553
e-mail: lynnlandes@earthlink.net
website: www.zerowasteamerica.org/index.html

Zero Waste America is an Internet-based environmental research organization specializing in the field of Zero Waste. Through its website, it provides information on legislative, legal, technical, environmental, health, and consumer issues. ZWA also specializes in information on US waste disposal issues, particularly the lack of a federal waste management plan, the use of disposal bans to legally stop waste disposal and imports, the long-proposed federal interstate waste legislation, waste data collection methodology, and applicable federal case law. Its website also offers photos, analysis of successful and unsuccessful recycling plans, and links to sources of news about waste, including electronic waste.

Bibliography

Books

Donald Bleiwas

Obsolete Computers: "Gold Mine," or High-Tech Trash? Washington, DC: US Geological Survey, 2001.

Kevin Brigden et al.

Recycling of Electronic Wastes in China and India: Workplace & Environmental Contamination. Exeter, UK: Greenpeace Research Laboratories, Greenpeace International, 2005.

Consumer Electronics Association

Market Research Report: Trends in CE Reuse, Recycle and Removal. Arlington, VA: CEA, 2008.

Dana Joel Gattuso

Mandated Recycling of Electronics: A Lose-Lose Proposition—Issue Analysis 2. Washington, DC: Competitive Enterprise Institute, 2005.

Elizabeth Grossman

High Tech Trash: Digital Devices, Hidden Toxics, and Human Health, 2nd ed. Washington, DC: Shearwater, 2007.

Linda Luther

Managing Electronic Waste—Issues with Exporting E-Waste. Washington, DC: Congressional Research Service, 2007.

Fred Pearce

Confessions of an Eco-Sinner. Boston: Beacon Press, 2008.

Randy Sarafan   *62 Projects to Make with a Dead
                        Computer (And Other Discarded
                        Electronics)*. New York: Workman,
                        2010.

Mark Schapiro   *Exposed: The Toxic Chemistry of
                        Everyday Products*. White River Jct.,
                        VT: Chelsea Green, 2007.

Silicon Valley   *Toxic Sweatshops: How UNICOR
Toxics Coalition,   Prison Recycling Harms Workers,
Prison Activist   Communities, the Environment, and
Resource Center,   the Recycling Industry*. San Francisco:
and the   Tides Foundation, 2006.
Electronics
TakeBack
Coalition

Ted Smith, David   *Challenging the Chip: Labor Rights
Sonnenfeld, and   and Environmental Justice in the
David Naguib   Global Electronics Industry*.
Pellow, eds.   Philadelphia: Temple University
                        Press, 2006.

US Government   *Electronic Waste: Strengthening the
Accountability   Role of the Federal Government in
Office   Encouraging Recycling and Reuse*.
                        Washington, DC: US GAO, 2005.

Periodicals

Greg Bolt   "Harvest Takes a Bite Out of
                        E-Waste—A UO Program Teaches
                        the Next Generation to Recycle
                        High-Tech Trash," *The
                        Register-Guard*, July 31, 2005.

Susan Carpenter   "Put E-Waste in Its Right Place—Old
                    TVs, Cellphones and Other
                    Electronics Don't Belong in the
                    Trash; They Should Be Recycled," *Los
                    Angeles Times*, January 9, 2010.

Chris Carroll   "High-Tech Trash—Will Your
                    Discarded TV End Up in a Ditch in
                    Ghana?," *National Geographic*,
                    January 2008.

China Daily   "Electronic Waste Poses Mounting
                    Challenge," April 6, 2005.

Mark Collins   "Cutting Back on Phone E-Waste,"
                    Boulder Daily Camera, July 13, 2010.

Consumer Reports "Think Green: Recycle Your Old
                    Electronics—States and Companies
                    Offer More Options for Consumers,"
                    April 2007.

Juliet Eilperin   "EPA Lets Electronic Waste Flow
                    Freely, GAO Report Says," *Washington
                    Post*, September 17, 2008.

Ben Elgin and   "E-Waste: The Dirty Secret of
Brian Grow   Recycling Electronics," *BusinessWeek*,
                    October 15, 2008.

Larry   "Trashed Tech: Where Do Old Cell
Greenemeier   Phones, TVs and PCs Go to Die?,"
                    Scientific American, November 29,
                    2007.

Walaika Haskins   "The Greening of Technology,"
                    TechNewsWorld, April 21, 2007.

Lily Huang   "Don't Toss Out That Old Gadget—Good Design Can Mean Dated Products Can Have Renewable Life Cycles," *Newsweek*, October 24, 2008.

Tim Johnson   "E-Waste Dump of the World," *Seattle Times*, April 9, 2006.

Liz Karan   "Environmental Internet and Phone Company Weighs in on E-Waste," *Environmental News Network*, May 2006.

Tom Knudson   "E-Waste Goes Overseas as Recyclers Comply with California Ban," *Los Angeles Times*, December 6, 2010.

Rachel Konrad   "Activists Push Recycling to Fight E-Waste," Associated Press, April 21, 2005.

Eve Mitchell   "Out with the Old High-Tech Gadgetry," *Contra Costa Times*, December 26, 2010.

Robert Mitchell   "Toxic Legacy—Improper Disposal of Obsolete IT Equipment Is Fast Becoming a Major Liability for Corporations," *Computer World*, February 2, 2004.

Christopher Moraff   "America's Slave Labor—Inmates Are Being Forced to Work in Toxic 'E-Waste' Sweatshops," *In These Times*, January 17, 2007.

New York Times   "Time to Deal with E-Waste," December 9, 2007.

Elizabeth Roche   "India's Poor Risk 'Slow Death'
                        Recycling E-Waste," *Agence France
                        Press*, July 7, 2010.

C.W. Schmidt   "E-Junk Explosion," *Environmental
                        Health Perspectives*, Vol. 110, No. 4,
                        April 2002.

Karl Schoenberger   "Many Old Computers Put to Use
                        Again, Study Finds," *San Jose Mercury
                        News*, April 27, 2005.

Giles Slade   "I-Waste," *Mother Jones*, March/April
                        2007.

Michael Standaert   "E-Waste Processing Poisons Health,
                        Environment," *IPS News*, May 3,
                        2010.

Bryan Walsh   "E-Waste Not," *Time*, January 8,
                        2009.

William Wright   "Waste Management of Consumer
                        Electronics Is a Growing Concern,"
                        Recycling, August 17, 2010.

Index